Steiff T.M.

Teddy Bears, Dolls, and Toys

with prices

A parade of
cuddly animals,
dolls, and toys from

Steiff

the famous maker of the Teddy Bear.

Jean Wilson and **Shirley Conway**

Cover Design and Layout: Heather Miller

Library of Congress
Catalog Number 82-050485

ISBN 0-87069-415-4

10 9 8 7 6 5 4 3

Published by

Wallace-Homestead Book Company
580 Water's Edge Road
Lombard, Illinois 60148

One of the ABC PUBLISHING abc Companies

Acknowledgments

Our first book, *100 Years of Steiff*, was published in 1980, the Steiff company's centennial year. Since that time, we have traveled to Germany for a first-hand inspection of the Steiff Museum and factory.

In cooperation with Margarete Steiff GmbH, we have assembled new information for this book, acknowledging that some dates are not exact, since the company did not keep complete records in their early years. We wish to thank the Steiff Company for supplying copies of old catalogs and for cooperating with us in every way.

We are indebted to Dr. and Mrs. Wolf Masuhr, who befriended and helped us with our translations, and to Monika Wietschorve, another new-found friend. Thanks, too, to Jorg Junginger, who taught two strangers from America a lot about Steiff toys.

We would also like to thank the following people for allowing us to use photographs of their collections and for other help:

Natalie Kutz
Kim Brewer
Seymour Lazerowitz
Ann Whitley
Lisa Palmer
Susan Hall
Gloria Zollinger
Eleanor Wood
Mary Julia Edwards
Marge Erwin

Mildred Stutz
Kay Hardman
Jim Mackey
Virginia Hopper
Kim Conway
Mary Jane Baxter
Donald Clemm
Tecla Powell
Mary Etta Kauffman
Heide Drewes

Contents

The Quaint Village of Giengen

The birthplace of Steiff toys seems a perfect setting for a product that has brought so much joy into the lives of so many people. Giengen on the Brenz, in the province of Bad Wurtemburg, Germany, is a tiny hamlet by today's standards, especially when you consider that it is the center of one of the most important toy industries in the world.

Giengen today is very similar to the Giengen that existed in 1847 when Margarete Steiff was born in a house in Lederstrasse, a former location of several leather tanneries. Housewives still go to market with baskets to buy their produce, and pigs are raised in a barn just off the main street.

Residents once again stroll up and down the main street, which for many years was used as a roadway for cars. The street was recently reinstated as a pedestrian walkway. Diners sit at tables alongside the street to drink beer from a local brewery (also in the heart of town), and the old church clock chimes every quarter-hour and strikes on the hour to remind visitors to Giengen that time does not really stand still.

Onion-top domes on an old church.

Birthplace of Margarete Steiff in Lederstrasse.

The town is enchanting and its residents are friendly. Visitors stay in the old Hotel Lamm in the center of town where Herr and Frau Hohnold take very good care of them. And for those interested in research, the Steiff Museum, which opened in 1980 when the company celebrated its centennial, is a fascinating place to visit. Many Steiff examples are displayed there tastefully in glass cases.

Street leading to City Hall.

Quaint buildings are everywhere.

Restored house in the village.

Aerial view of Giengen showing Steiff factory (foreground left).

Renovated main street.

Dr. Herbert Zimmerman, President, Margarete Steiff GmbH.

Hans Otto Steiff, President, Steiff Holding Company.

Dieter Kaiser, Export Manager for Steiff GmbH.

Dieter Olszewski, Marketing Manager, Steiff GmbH.

Jorg Junginger, Director of Development, Steiff Company. Also in charge of the Steiff Museum.

Margarete Steiff.

Behind the Scenes

A designer draws the toy.

A woman snips the pattern by hand.

Sewing is tedious work.

A tour of the Steiff Company is a reminder that true quality is only achieved by constant supervision and meticulous handwork. While the quality of Steiff toys has not changed over the years, the newer toys are noticeably different from the older ones collectors seek. There are good reasons for the changes, though, and in some cases the newer toys are actually better than the older ones. Though a teddy bear collector may look for humps, mohair, dangling arms and shaped legs, a small child is really better off with a soft, cuddly toy that is washable and fire-resistant. Fortunately, there seems to be room for both products in today's market — the old mohair and felt toys as well as the newer synthetic ones.

Not surprisingly, huge bolts of mohair and synthetic fabrics with which the toys are covered are found at the Steiff factory. Patterns are still painted onto the fabrics using large brushes, with 80 percent of the cutting done by hand. A factory in Tunisia handles cutting and sewing, but the toys are all constructed in Germany and Austria.

Women still snip shapes with scissors much as they have done for one hundred years. In the Steiff Museum there is a sewing machine similar to the one Margarete Steiff would have used back in 1880. The intricate sewing needed to stitch a tiny leg or ear is still tedious work. Machines are operated manually by women in the factory. A few special machines sew complicated patterns automatically, but these, too, are for the most part operated by hand.

One explanation for the durability of Steiff toys is the method used for sewing seams. The machines are programmed to sew a few stitches and then reverse to tie knots periodically. These frequent knots prevent seams from coming loose.

A difficult task, although most of us would not consider it so, is turning the fabric for a toy or doll inside out once the seams are sewn. Just imagine how difficult it would be to invert the leg of a small teddy bear. The fabric is turned by attaching a leg to special rods made just for this purpose. The procedure, although it sounds simple, requires delicate handwork.

Eyes are attached to Steiff toys very firmly by a device called a "starlock." Tests have shown that the power of nine kilopounds will not remove them once they are attached. Eyelashes are inserted at just the right angle once the eyes are in place.

Stuffing the toys.

Joints are made of nails and special washers inserted into a machine that secures them, then cuts off the sharp tips. The process is very complicated, and it is easy to understand why small animals are no longer jointed. It takes too much precision and time to warrant the cost.

Most Steiff toys today are stuffed with polyester fiber or polyurethane foam, but excelsior is still used occasionally (in the Mecki arms and in the life-sized animals). It is illegal to use excelsior in items used strictly as toys, but it is permissible in collectors' items, such as the Centennial Bear and other display pieces.

Sewing the nose.

Excelsior is flammable and cannot be washed, but it is also not used as much as it was in the past because few workmen will take on the difficult job of stuffing this material into the dolls or animals. It takes great strength, especially in the large animals, and very few people today are willing to learn the art.

More frequently, toys are stuffed by blowers that insert foam particles into the various shapes, with each toy weighed to ensure uniformity. Molded polyurethane forms, when used, are inserted into animals by a special pneumatic machine. Bendable wires have replaced joints in some toys. Final seams are still sewn by hand, however.

An artist with an airbrush.

Touches of color are applied by artists with air brushes in just the right spots to look natural. Paws are sewn by hand and machines sew the noses. Each toy is checked to be sure it is perfect. Only then is the button in the ear attached.

The sturdy metal frames used for the life-sized and riding animals are very impressive, and the quality Margarete Steiff insisted on one hundred years ago is evident today in the entire factory. The present system of production has actually changed very little in the past one hundred years. Margarete Steiff GmbH continues to prosper. Let's hope the company never stops producing the toys that children of all ages love so dearly.

Margarete Steiff's trademark: a button in the ear.

The Parade Begins

Margarete Steiff's elephant pincushion.

Pages from Richard Steiff's sketchbook.

It isn't often that tragedy brings good fortune, but in the case of Margarete Steiff, that might be an exception. Although she contracted polio as a young child, she later started her own business as a dressmaker and eventually became a toy magnate. Her determination to become independent of her family as a result of her handicap prompted Margarete to open her own shop as a seamstress, using products from her uncle's felt factory to make clothing for women.

The business was successful, and about the time that she hired several helpers, she had already conceived the idea of making a novelty pincushion in the shape of an elephant. This was in 1880, the birthdate of Steiff toys and the beginning of soft plush animals.

Her nephews and their friends enjoyed playing with the elephant pincushion so much that Margarete made other animals, too — camels, monkeys, donkeys, horses, and pigs. Her brother Fritz took the toys to a country fair and sold every one, convincing Margarete that she should consider making toys as well as dresses.

In 1893 an agent represented Steiff at the Leipzig Toy Fair for the first time, and a catalog was printed. International fame didn't come to Steiff, however, until the invention of a small bear with a movable head and joints, suggested by Margarete's nephew Richard.

Richard was truly an artist, as a glimpse of his sketchbook reveals. He had watched several bears in an animal show at Stüttgart, sketching them from various angles. When he first suggested to his aunt that they make a new type of bear, she was not overly enthusiastic. She had already produced bears standing on four legs as well as a dancing bear on two legs. Richard's bear, however, would be different. His would be the first bear with movable joints, similar to a doll. It could be dressed, cuddled, and loved, he said — and it has been ever since. Margarete and Richard covered their bear in a realistic-looking fur fabric made of wool mohair. The 1903 catalog, issued in June, lists for the first time, a "bar," or baby bear, fifty-five centimeters long (or about two feet).

Pages from Richard Steiff's sketchbook.

Prototype of gray bear made by Richard Steiff.

The Steiff Company has in its possession the original prototype of this first teddy bear. It was given to Richard Steiff's mother-in-law, kept by the family all these years, then given back to the factory in 1942 as proof that Steiff did make a teddy bear before the 1903 catalog.

When Richard's bears were first taken to the Leipzig Toy Fair, an American buyer ordered 3,000 of them. The American Dream is to strive for the White House, and that was to be the destiny of these little bears. Legend has it that the caterer in charge of decorating tables for a party for the daughter of President Theodore Roosevelt decided to use the bears as his theme. Since the President was known for his big-game hunting, the bears were dressed in various types of hunting gear and arranged on the tables. Comments by guests and the President reportedly led to the nickname "Teddy's bears." About the same time, a cartoon appeared in newspapers depicting the President's refusal to shoot a bear cub. In succeeding catalogs, the "bar" was transformed to "teddy."

The success of the teddy bear was to make Margarete Steiff's company internationally known. But Margarete wanted more. She also wanted her toys to be recognized for their quality by a standard trademark.

In 1905 the famous "button in ear" was added to every Steiff toy. The first buttons were small tin circles that resembled pewter. The name was raised in block letters as illustrated. The familiar script Steiff logo was not seen until 1932, and it was about this same time that the button changed to a shiny, possibly chrome one. Brass buttons were not used until 1980.

This angle shows the distinctive hump.

Teddy bears dressed in hunting garb.

Steiff logos.

1897

STEIFF - ORIGINAL - MARKE

1927

STEIFF - ORIGINAL - MARKE

1950

KNOPF IM OHR

1971

Other company trademarks that help determine age are the cardboard tags that were attached to the bodies of the toys. One of the oldest toys in the Steiff Museum is a standing bear with a round cardboard tag. On this tag is a rendering of Margarete Steiff's first elephant with a curving trunk encircling her initials. This trademark, which first appeared in 1897, was used until the success of the teddy bear led to a squared-off bear's head as the trademark.

This bear with the smiling mouth was changed to a bear with a rounded head and a different mouth in about 1950. The present banner logo was added in 1971.

Rectangular paper tags have also been attached with the button. It is possible that the first ones were white. Red tags were used beginning about 1926. There is evidence of an orange tag used on a Mickey Mouse doll from the 1930s. The yellow tag has been used since 1931, and the fabric yellow tag of today was introduced in 1980.

Many of the toys in the Steiff Museum do not have buttons or tags, since they were never sold, but kept as samples or models. It is possible that old supplies of buttons and the like were used after World War II when materials were not available.

The button with the printed Steiff logo was probably used until about 1932. However, there are rayon plush animals with this button known to exist, and these animals were only made after World War II. For a short period after World War II, anything made in Western Germany bore the tag "Made in U.S. Zone Germany." Tags with these words will occasionally be found on Steiff toys as a further clue to dating.

The earliest Steiff toys were made entirely of felt, with felt shearings or wool fibers used as stuffing. Velvet and plush coverings were mentioned in early catalogs, but this plush is not the same as mohair plush, which was not used until the teddy bear of 1903.

During World War I, when fabrics were hard to obtain, several new coverings were tried. A material woven from a plant called die brennessel (nettle) and a paper plush were used on a teddy bear, but were highly unsatisfactory because they were not durable.

World War II caused further experimentation with coverings such as oilcloth and rayon plush. Both were not the quality one expects from Steiff, however. Excelsior was the major stuffing used until hygiene and safety laws forced a move to nonflammable and washable polyester products.

The earliest eyes were black shoe buttons. Glass eyes were used quite early, particularly in the dolls, and plastic replaced the glass after World War II. Wheels on animals were made of metal until 1913, when wooden wheels were added to the line. Rubber-rimmed metal wheels date from about 1925, but appeared consistently after World War II. In the 1925 catalog, examples of all three types of wheels are shown.

Dolls are listed in the first catalogs, but changed over the years as explained later in the section on dolls. Steiff also made other novelty items such as coffee warmers, egg warmers, bottle covers, rattles, and hats that look like chickens. Wooden toys were produced until 1971, and during the 1920s Steiff even made metal cars. The roloplan, a type of kite, was added to the line in 1908 and contributed to the company's success.

The years after World War II were the most profitable for the Steiff Company, which continued under the direction of Margarete's five nephews after her death in 1909. A line of miniatures was promoted to make collecting toys a hobby for many children who were now parents themselves. Reclining toys were introduced in the mid-1950s and became especially popular with truck drivers who took them on their long trips as companions.

The Teddy Baby, a special type of standing teddy bear, became a fixture in the line from 1929 on and was made in a variety of sizes. Hand puppets were produced from about 1912, as well as hanging crib toys and marionettes. Steiff had the first license to produce a Mickey Mouse doll with the permission of Walt Disney in the early 1930s.

Life-sized animals have been used for many years as display pieces, and some of these are highly prized today. The first animated display was created in 1912, and many more were made in later years for various toy fairs and Steiff showrooms, as well as for some department stores.

Brennessel elephant from World War I.

Paper plush teddy bear from World War I.

Army mule and Navy goat.

Animated display of Steiff toys.

Country Mouse and house.

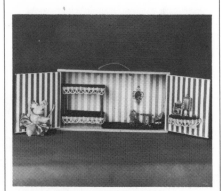

City Mouse and house.

It is through a study of the various coverings used on Steiff toys, the trademarks, buttons, and sophistication of construction that the age of a toy can be determined.

Many novelty items that did not originate from the Steiff factory have turned up in the research for this book. Individual stores or organizations apparently purchased certain pieces in quantity and adapted them for their own use. A mule wearing an Army sweater and a goat wearing the emblem of Navy are examples. Obviously, these were sold to promote the football rivalry between the two teams. F.A.O. Schwarz has featured many specialty items in its catalogs, such as the Country Mouse and City Mouse, which came complete with their own houses.

It would be impossible to track down every item that has come out of the Steiff factory, but each year brings new information about the company since its inauspicious beginning more than one hundred years ago.

Richard Steiff, designer of the teddy bear.

Paul Steiff, Margarete Steiff's nephew.

Franz Steiff, another nephew.

Margarete Steiff's nephew, Otto.

Nephew Hugo Steiff.

Women hard at work making
Steiff toys in 1926.

Steiff factory in 1920.

Steiff factory, 1960.

The Truth About Steiff Dolls

To fully understand the dolls made by Margarete Steiff's toy company, it is helpful to divide them into different categories. A few of the dolls that appear in the 1897 catalog are believed to have bisque heads purchased from another company and are not typical of any others made by Steiff.

The first dolls made completely by Steiff were the caricature type. The definition of caricature is "exaggeration by means of ludicrous distortion of parts," and this is characteristic of these dolls, which were made entirely of felt.

They included policemen, soldiers, clowns, bakers, farmers, musicians, school children, housewives, and ladies. Their faces are quite different from the beautiful bisque dolls which were popular during the same era, and they have noticeable seams running down their middles.

Many consider the caricature dolls ugly. They have grotesque features such as big noses, large chins, big ears, skinny faces, big chests, pot bellies, stick legs, large buttocks, and exaggerated hands and feet.

But beauty is in the eye of the beholder, and no one is perfect. People come in different shapes and sizes and so do Steiff dolls. Perhaps you will recognize a feature of one of your loved ones in these dolls, and that will make it more lovable to you.

These dolls are truly unique works of art, and most collectors think that they are the only dolls made by Steiff; however, there are seven other categories, some made during the same period as the caricature type.

The most appealing of the early Steiff dolls are the adorable children. They bear such names as Otto, Olga, Karl, and Felix. Instead of grotesque features, these dolls have the fat, rosy cheeks typical of German children. Their costumes are made of wool, felt, and cotton, with leather and felt shoes and accessories of different types — school slates, books, skis, backpacks, and sleds.

These dolls first appeared in catalogs from 1913 and were only made until 1930. Gnome and elf dolls appeared as early as 1905, with the earliest ones made entirely of felt with seamed faces. They also had the large feet of the caricature type. Later gnomes were made with rubber faces.

In 1922 a most unusual doll with a celluloid head was designed by a man named Schlopsnies for Steiff. The heads were manufactured by the Rohlinge Von Schildkrot Company and bear a turtle mark. The felt bodies were made by Steiff and had seams down the front and back.

The unique feature of this doll is its face, which was painted from the inside, giving the complexion a beautiful apricot color. Because of the special "aprico process," the doll's face could be washed over and over without wearing away the colors. Most collectors have never seen this doll, and no collectors' catalog has ever shown it. Perhaps it has been attributed to the Schildkrot Company instead of Steiff.

A major difference between this doll and the earlier Steiff felt dolls is that the arms are not jointed. They are stitched to the shoulders. The legs and head are jointed like the others.

Beginning in 1930, Steiff produced dolls with pressed-felt faces and stuffed-felt bodies. For the first time, their dolls had mohair wigs that could be washed and combed. The felt was molded onto a base shaped to define the facial features. This eliminated the need for seams; thus the faces appeared smooth and more appealing. Names like Rudi, Else, Lisl, Dorus, Rita, and Brigette were given to these dolls, which were often made in pairs with costumes typical of different countries, such as Holland or Austria.

Some of these dolls had the cardboard tags attached with their names and plastic bracelets with the button and tag attached. They were dressed in beautiful costumes with separate shoes. Pressed-felt dolls are still made today, but by a different process. The earlier pressed-felt dolls were produced until 1952. Though not as old as the caricature dolls, these pressed-felt dolls would be an excellent addition to any doll collection.

Animals dressed as humans were advertised in the very first catalog and are still being made by Steiff today. From gorillas to teddy bears to dogs, the variety is endless. The age of these dolls can only be determined through study of their construction, buttons, and tags, but they are dolls that have a lot of appeal and deserve attention.

Gnomes and elves were mentioned earlier because they were made as early as 1905, but after World War II Steiff made a different type of elf doll. The Mecki family was made in the 1950s. They were replicas of hedgehogs dressed as a man, woman, girl, and boy. Their faces were made of rubber; their hair was made of a coarse, brushy material. They had felt, jointed bodies.

In addition to the Mecki family, a group of elves named Lucki, Pucki, and Gucki were made. These dolls had felt, jointed bodies and felt clothing. Their faces were also made of rubber, and they had mohair beards. A Santa Claus with the same construction was made in various sizes at about the same time. The other categories are the Kewpie, about which we know very little, and the radiator caps with dolls attached.

Dolls continue to be made by Steiff. Most can be seen in stores and new catalogs, thus new dolls are not included in this book for collectors, although there are a few examples in the price guide section.

Caricature Dolls

Felt dolls with exaggerated features, seamed faces and bodies, dressed in clothing of felt and other materials, some with added accessories.

Made: 1903-1914 (A few were made in 1925.)
Size: various
Materials: felt, plush, velvet
Mark: tin button in ear with printed logo
Head: seam down middle of face and back of head; painted features, mohair wigs, glass eyes
Body: stuffed felt, sewn both front and back, jointed at head, shoulders, and hips, fingers sewn and stitched with thumb free, feet extra long for standing

Animal Dolls

Animals in upright positions, dressed like people.

Made: 1897 on
Size: various
Materials: felt, plush, velvet, mohair, some on wooden wheels
Clothes: cotton, felt
Mark: metal button in ear, cardboard tags on some
Head: seam down sides of face, glass eyes, painted and sewn features
Body: stuffed felt, mohair plush, velvet, jointed head, shoulders and hips, sewn both front and back

Acrobat caricature doll showing seams and joints.

Back view of caricature doll.

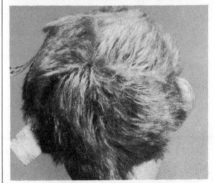

Back of head showing wig, tag in ear, seams, and joints.

Animal dolls dressed as people.

Early Children Dolls

Felt dolls portraying children of various types without exaggerated features, often dressed in native costumes of various countries.

Made: 1913-1930
Size: various
Material: felt
Clothes: cotton, felt, leather, velvet, wool, leather shoes
Mark: metal button in ear (probably tin with printed logo)
Head: stuffed felt, seam down middle of face, stationary glass eyes, painted features, mohair wigs
Body: stuffed felt, seams both front and back, jointed head, shoulders, and hips, feet in proportion to body

Gnomes, Elves, Mecki Family, Santa Claus

Dolls made of various materials portraying imaginary characters, some of the caricature type.

Made: 1905 on
Size: various
Materials: felt, rubber, mohair plush, early ones all felt, rubber after about 1953
Mark: metal button in ear
Head: (early) felt with seams down middle of face; (1930s) pressed-felt with mohair wigs; (1953) rubber, mohair wigs and beards, glass stationary eyes, painted features
Body: stuffed felt, jointed head, shoulders, and hips, extra large feet on early specimens

Early children dolls.

Gnomes and elves.

Schlopsnies

Doll with felt body and molded, celluloid head painted from inside.

Made: 1922-1925
Size: 16″
Materials: celluloid, felt
Mark: blue plastic tag with bear's head marked "Steiff Schlopsnies," cardboard tag on clothing, red plastic bracelet on arm
Head: made by Rohlinge Von Schildkrot of Germany with the turtle mark of Rheinische Gummi und Celluloid Fabrik Company; crown cut for painting from inside and re-glued; painted hair and features, eyes recessed and painted
Body: stuffed felt, seams both front and back, jointed head and hips, arms sewn to shoulders

Note: The 1934 catalog shows a similar doll made with a celluloid head, but with stationary glass eyes. The hands are mitten-type felt. The body is fully jointed. The ad states "DRP zum USA Patent." It is not referred to as a Schlopsnies.

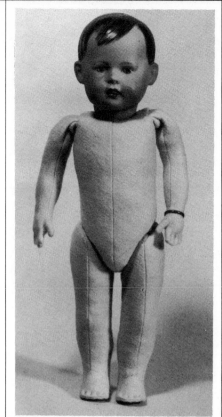

Front view of Schlopsnies doll.

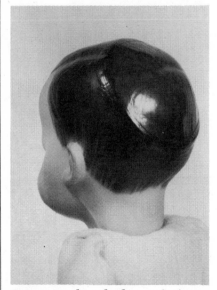

Crown replaced after painting head.

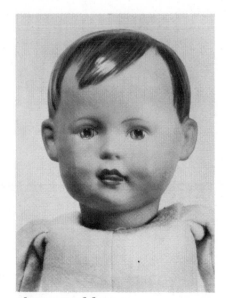

Close-up of face.

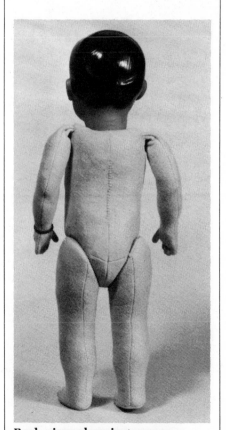

Back view showing seams.

Kewpie Dolls

Felt baby dolls made in the style of a kewpie.

Made: 1925 to ?
Materials: felt, mohair
Mark: button (?)
Head: seam down middle of face, side-glancing stationary glass eyes, painted features, mohair fringe on top of bald head
Body: felt, head, shoulders, and hips jointed, wearing only booties

Note: This doll made its first and last appearance in the 1925 Steiff catalog. It was never advertised again after that year.

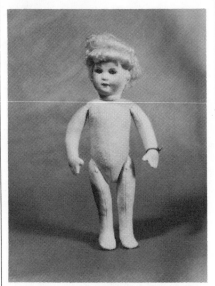

Pressed-felt face.

Steiff kewpie doll with other toys.

Front view of pressed-felt doll.

Pressed-Felt Dolls

Dolls made entirely of felt with molded felt heads and mohair wigs.

Made: 1930-1952
Sizes: 14″ and 17″
Material: felt
Clothes: cotton, felt, wool, velvet
Mark: wrist bracelet with button, name tag on clothing
Head: pressed felt, seam at back of neck, glass stationary eyes, painted features
Body: stuffed felt, seams both front and back, jointed head and hips, arms sewn to shoulders

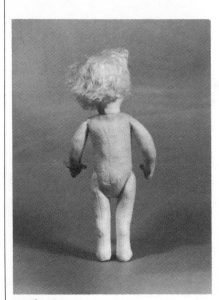

Back view.

Radiator Caps for Automobiles

Animals and dolls attached to radiator caps as decoration.

Made: 1913 to ?
Sizes: 15½″ (man); 8″ (monkey)
Material: felt (man); mohair and felt (monkey)
Clothes: felt
Mark: button in ear
Body: mohair, jointed, felt face (monkey); all felt (man); both
      attached to radiator caps

Bottom view.

Radiator caps in upright
position.

Cheers!

Ideal teddy bear from Smithsonian.

Anthony Andrews and Jeremy Irons with Aloysius. Photograph courtesy of Granada Television.

The most gratifying thing that resulted from the publication of our first book, *100 Years of Steiff*, was the many letters received from Steiff lovers all over the country.

Young children who were just starting collections wrote with questions; adults who had played with Steiff toys as children told about their experiences. The message that came through loud and clear was that once you own a Steiff toy, you always love it.

We also had some correspondence with the Smithsonian Institution about the teddy bear that supposedly belonged to Theodore Roosevelt (it turns out that the bear was the original made by Ideal Toy Company of New York) and with Granada Television concerning the bear used in the production of "Brideshead Revisited." Aloysius, the teddy bear treasured by Sebastian in the story, belonged to Peter Bull, the English teddy bear connoisseur, and is indeed a Steiff.

Finally, for collectors who did not read our first book, we would like to repeat the suggestions about caring and cleaning for old Steiff toys.

Cleaning Steiff animals is easy with a vacuum and sweeper attachments. If toys or animals have mites, moths, or silverfish, place them in a box and spray them with a bug killer, then leave them overnight. If animals or dolls are soiled, use a foam rug cleaner. Woolite is good, since many of the animals are made of mohair, which is a woolen fabric. Spray only enough to cover the animal lightly. Let it dry, then clean with your sweeper attachment. Brush in a circular motion with a soft brush to bring up the nap.

Many of the animals can be wiped clean with a damp cloth and mild soap or detergent. Never put your animals in a dryer or bright sunlight. This might damage the color or fabric. Once cleaned, let them dry at room temperature after lightly wiping with a bath towel.

A Steiff collector illustrates her collection. Illustration courtesy of Lisa Palmer.

Steiff murals in a child's nursery. Photographs and murals courtesy of Heide L. Drewes.

Reviewing the Line

Thirteen years after the first elephant pincushion was made by Margarete Steiff, her company published its first catalog. By this time, her business had grown from a small seamstress shop to a commercial enterprise with an agent at the Leipzig Toy Fair.

This 1893 catalog shows camels, horses with wagons and sleighs, donkeys, clowns, elephants, dogs, giraffes, apes, rabbits, cats, mice, sheep, a bowling game, animals on bicycles, pincushions, penwipers, and two dolls. The dolls, which were listed as a Tyrolean and child and apparently had bisque heads, were not made by Steiff, but could have been dressed by them.

By 1897 many new items were added to the catalog, including a doll that revolved on a music box and several varieties of birds. Several farmyard animals (a billy goat, an ox, and a pig), a fox, squirrels, and a lion were also new. The dolls now included a farmer and wife, a sailor and wife, a gardener and wife, a woman, a boy, a clown, and a windup child. There were rattles, assortments of small animals, and even an ape in a moon rocker. A kangaroo, a reindeer, and a dachshund were introduced in 1898, the first year the elephant trademark was in evidence.

An advertisement of new items dated 1903-1904 shows several caricature dolls, mostly of policemen and a Negro. All have the large feet typical of the early Steiff dolls. It is this catalog that proves Steiff created a teddy bear before 1903. In order to include it in their catalog, which came out in June, it had to have been conceived much earlier. Though it is pictured, it had not yet acquired the name "teddy," but was listed as "bar," which means bear in German.

The 1905 catalog had many illustrations of children holding teddy bears. The size of each bear is evident by comparison with the sizes of the children. The list of offerings was quite extensive, with most items made in a variety of sizes. *Knopf im Ohr* (button in ear) was first used as a trademark in this catalog. Dolls were limited to policemen, clowns, and a few soldiers, but only thirteen varieties were listed.

Neuheiten 1903-04.

per Dtzg

		Häng-Taub M	Häng-Schwalb M		
Aff 60 P B	Bär 55 P B	Bär 8 M	Kater M	Rad-Fex	
Neger Fusbaler	Ele 14 T (grösser s. Liste)	Esl 22 P (grösser s. Liste)	Lam 22 T ohne R (grösser s. Liste)	Kaz 14 siz T (gröss. s. L.)	
Police 35 Engl.	Sau 14 T (grösser s. Liste)	Ele 22 P (grösser s. Liste)	Fox 17 siz T (grösser s. Liste)	Kaz 14 T (gröss. s. L.)	
Has 14 ren T (grösser s. Liste)	Ueberdax M	Police 35 französ.	Kaz 12 lig T (grösser s. Liste)		
Löw 14 lig M	Eich 5 M Blatt	Ox 14 M	Postman 50 Engl.	Postman 35 Engl.	Police 50 Engl.	Frosch mit Ruder 35
Frosch 5 M Nad	Hen Brut M	Taub 10 M Nad	Fussballer 35	Kamel 14 M	Neger 35

Umwenden!

Catalog page showing first Steiff bear.

1920
STEIFF
GIENGEN AN DER BRENZ

The first catalog that refers to the "bar" as "teddy" was dated 1908. One bear actually wears a shirt with the name on it. The small bear was first introduced in the 1903 issue, but in the five-year interim, costumes, leashes, and even a teddy that turned somersaults were added. Rockers could now be ordered with certain animals, including a horse.

The 1913 catalog had a cover designed by Schlopsnies, who later created the unique celluloid dolls described in the doll portion of this book. The 1913 issue boasts of grand prizes won in St. Louis in 1904 and in Brussels in 1910 and advertises showrooms in many cities throughout the world. The speedaway monkey on wooden wheels first appeared in 1913.

Most of the caricature dolls pictured in this book were also displayed in the 1913 catalog, which was the last catalog with such a large assortment of dolls. Wooden accessories such as bunk beds and school desks were shown, as well as egg warmers (called "hide a gift" by the company), chicken hats, the roloplan (a kite designed by Richard Steiff), and a zebra. Wooden wheels on some of the small toys were shown for the first time.

The first catalog after World War I was probably issued in 1920, and it is much smaller than previous ones. Since most of the caricature dolls were eliminated from the line in 1914, only a few child-type dolls were shown, plus the roloplan and some wooden furniture for children.

By 1925 the selection was much larger, especially in dolls. The dolls no longer had seamed faces. Most had pressed-felt faces, except for the Schlopsnies doll with a celluloid head.

Cardboard tags were added to the chests of animals in the late 1920s. These tags usually bore the name of the particular toy and are often found intact. If the tag is missing from an old toy, one can sometimes find the thread where it was originally attached.

Teddy Babies were introduced in 1929, and they continued to be made for many years. The 1932 catalog shows wooden trucks, trains, scooters, and cars made of metal. Catalogs were printed in 1937-1938 and 1939-1940, but the first one to appear after World War II was not issued until 1948.

This catalog is really just a small pamphlet printed in black and white with only a few animals offered in one or two sizes. Mohair plush was not mentioned in the descriptions, and, from the pictures, it is obvious that many were made from an inferior material, which was all that was available at the time. Toys made of this fabric (a type of rayon plush) can be dated fairly accurately.

It was after the war that the small miniature animals became so popular with children and adults who wanted to accumulate a collection without spending too much money. Some were made of wool, but the better ones were made of mohair. The variety was endless now, and certain animals were made only for a short time if they did not prove to be good sellers.

Catalogs from 1949 on were quite extensive. Innovations such as the dwarfs called Gucki, Lucki, and Pucki, Santa Claus, and the Mecki hedgehog dolls gave new impetus to the Steiff line. These dolls had rubber faces and felt bodies, unlike the earlier dolls made entirely of felt. The Zotty bear and baboon were just some of the other new items of the 1950s.

The 1950s were big years for Steiff, especially in America, and this prosperity continued until the 1970s, when the uncertain money situation throughout the world took its toll on European markets in general. The high cost of the products, in conjunction with the unstable American dollar, made it very risky for American merchants to place orders for European products. Steiff toys were no exception.

With recent improvements in this area, Steiff toys are once again readily available in many American stores, and the increasing interest in collecting older Steiff has spurred new enthusiasm for the collectors' items and new products.

The 1980 Centennial Bear was an overwhelming success. With 6,000 made for the European market and 5,000 for America, the value of the bear, which sold new for $150, has more than doubled in three years. The 1981 Mama and Baby Bear have also been quite popular, and the new white teddies and the Teddy Bear Tea Party are especially desirable for those who want the old types of bears for their collections.

The Margaret Strong Teddy Bear, which was issued in October of 1982 to coincide with the opening of her museum in Rochester, New York, is an exact replica of one of the earliest bears made by Steiff. It was copied from Mrs. Strong's own childhood bear and is offered in several sizes.

On the following pages is an assortment of items advertised in various Steiff catalogs. It is impossible to show every toy, but these samples may be helpful in establishing the age of other Steiff products.

1893

488   499   522   531s   539s   549   533

577   585 589   586   591   590   596s   600   602s   607 606 654   551

636   632   641   645   651   657   658   660   659   662   696   697   707

557 556   550   561

558   560   565   609 – 15   617   625   623

708   710   711   721

1897

405   415   431   447   456   464

403   423 I   413   429   444 II

472   480   460 I   507

For children only the best is good enough! True to this principle, I am now sending out my 5th Illustrated Price List.

The greatly extended patronage which my business continues to recieve, especially during the past year, together with

Increasing export sales, and the demand generally for further numbers of every kind of animal, prompt me to enlarge my business and to very materially increase and improve my stuffed toy animals, both as regards artistic and technical execution. My new catalogue now contains

About 50% of novelties.

As to the indestructible character, durability, originality and popularity of my goods, I have received a large number of testimonials from my customers, a fact speaking sufficiently for itself. I therefore only here briefly describe the

Registered constructions of the animals.

The stuff-covering consists of best quality felt or plush, especially manufactured for the purpose, and as far as possible protected against moths.

The stuffing is light, soft and pure (no sawdust, animal hair etc.).

The strong metal frame serves to hold the form and to import the astonishing bearing strength to the larger animals.

The light weight in proportion to the high value involves only small duty and low charges for transit.

My trade-mark "M. St. Elefant", should be particularly noted, in order to guard against worthless imitations, such as have been put upon the market of late.

Leading Felt Toy Manufactory of Germany.

1905

(52) 1135

BU 22

FU 35

AL 35

GA 50

(64) 1528,0

GR 35

HO 35

KA 35

KO 43

(66) 5322,1

(46) 6522

PLF 35

PLA 35

PLA 50

PLE 35

PLE 50

44) 1235

44) 3222

MJ 35

PSE 35

PSE 50

SOE 35

SOE 50

1905

(10) 5150

(12) 1322

(12) 5317,1

(22) 2128

(12) 5343,1

5322,1

(10) 5235

(14) 1343

(24) 5235,½

(10) 5335

(20) 1135

(36) 4428|6

(24) 1225

(10) 5350

(20) 1228

(36) 4522,6

(20) 5222,1

1908

1908

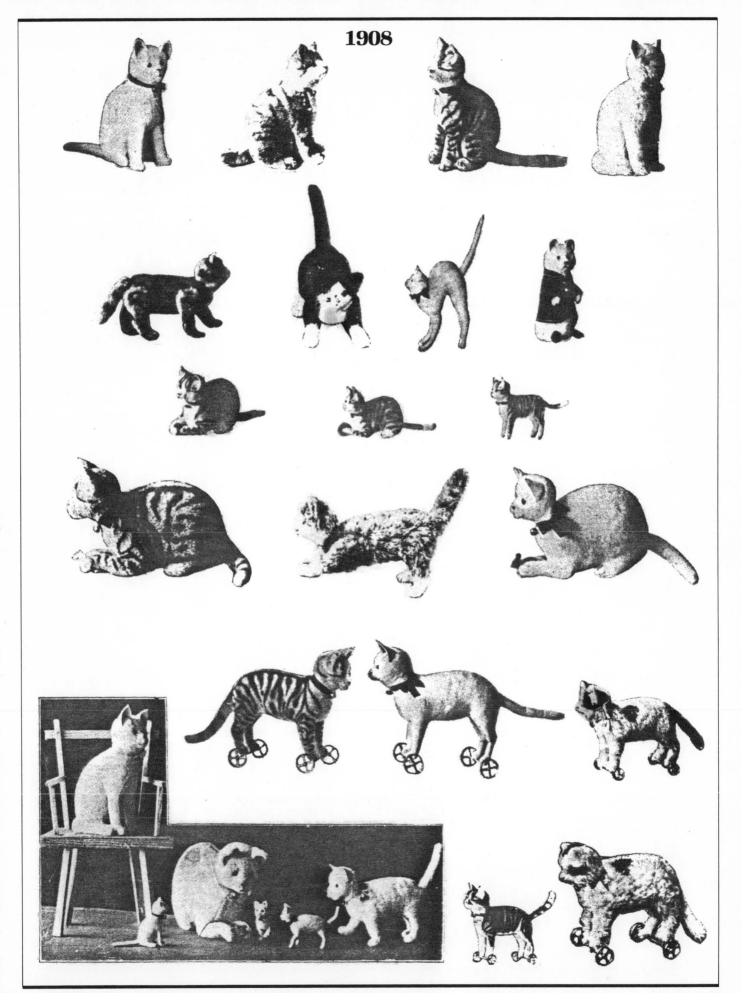

1908

1913

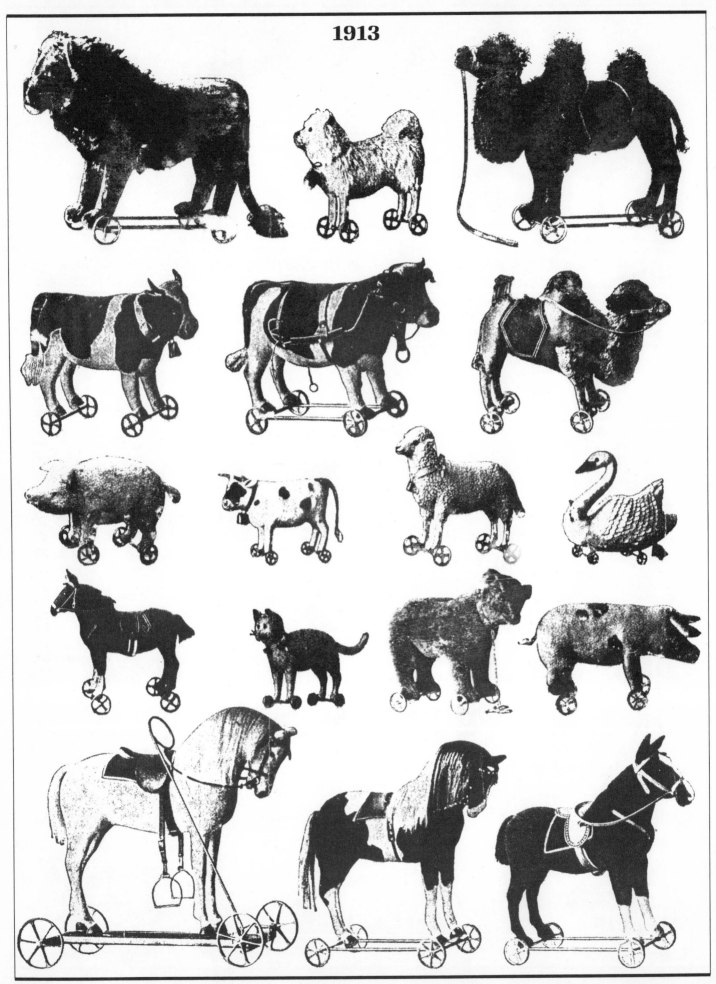

1913

1913

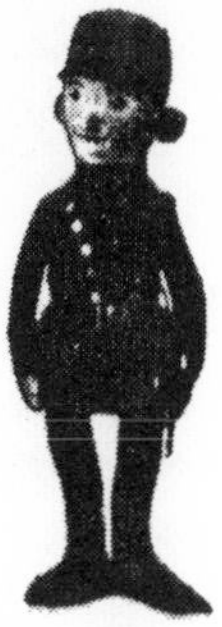

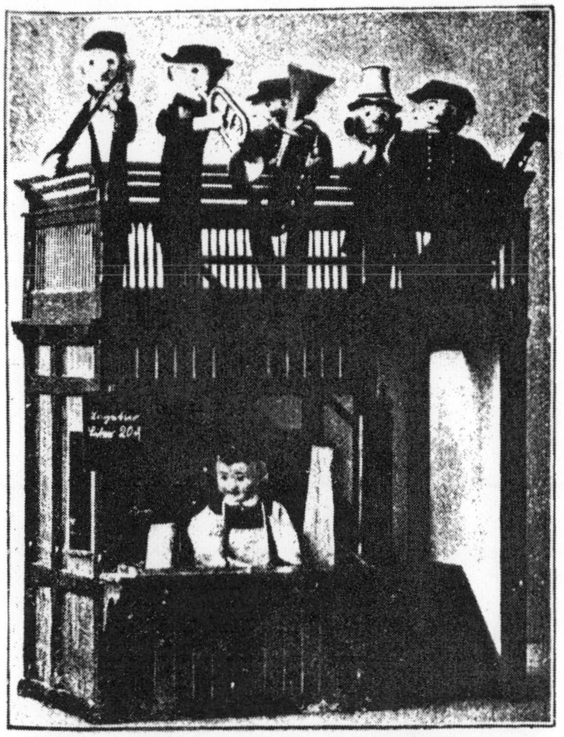

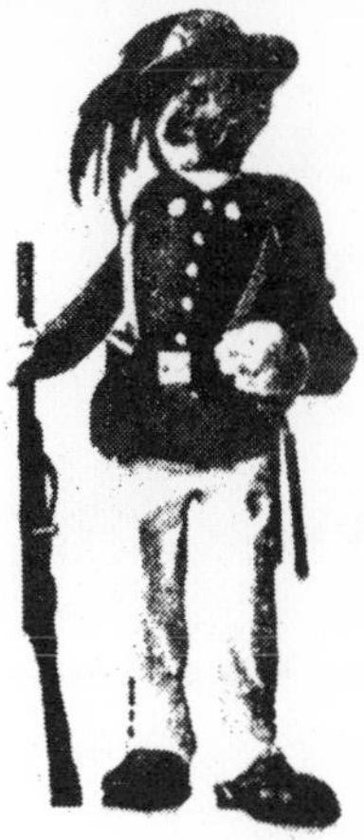

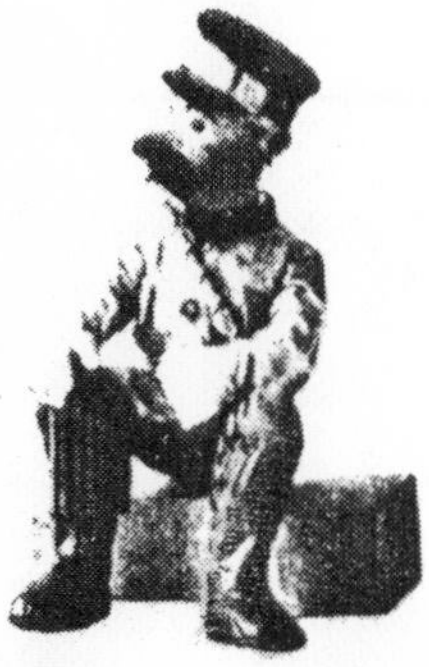

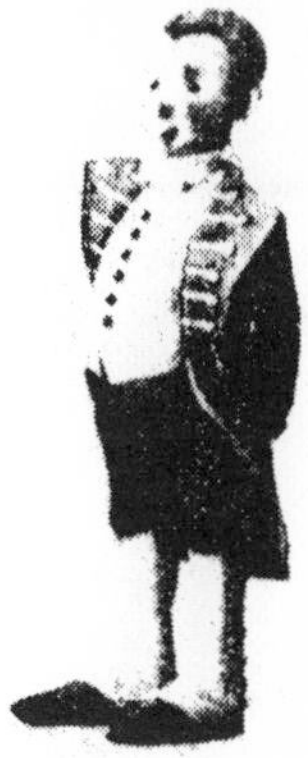

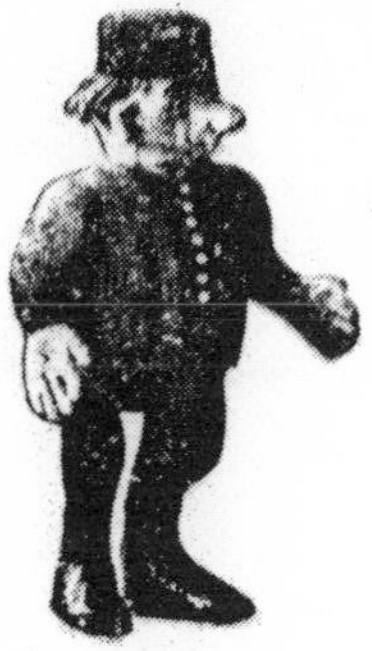

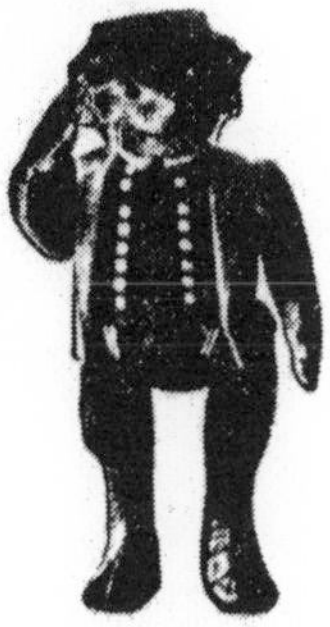

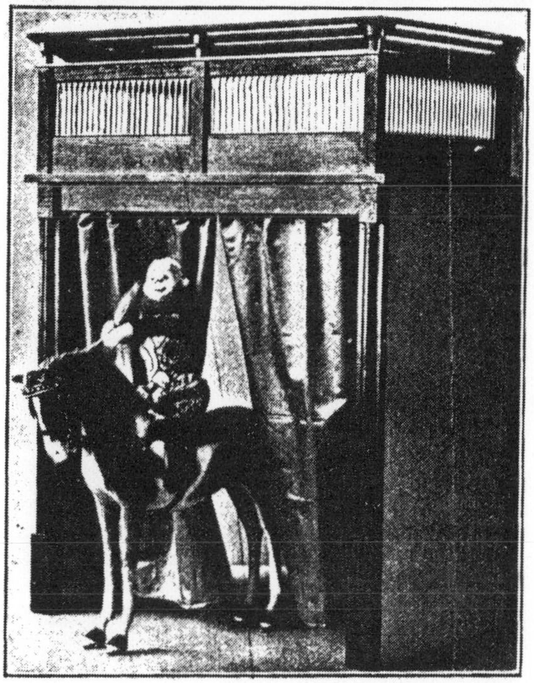

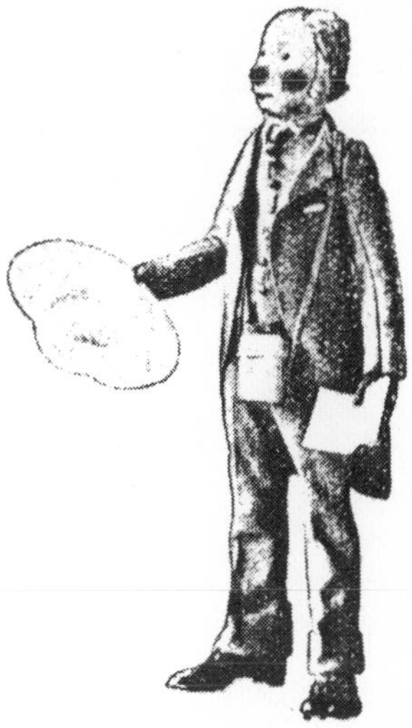

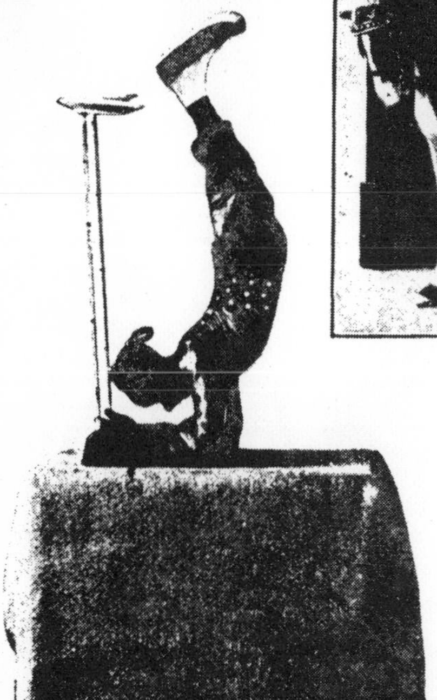

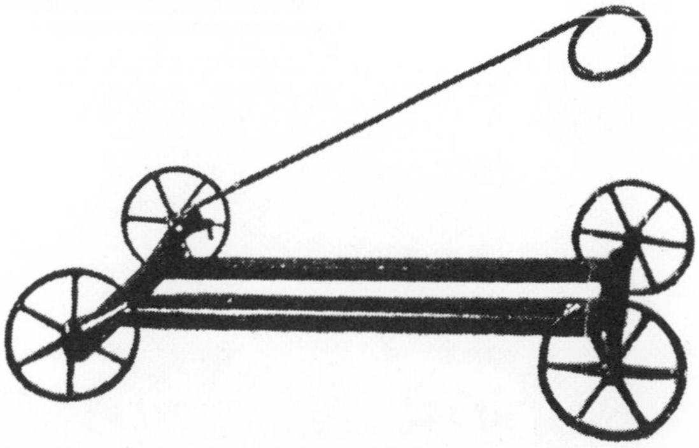

1920

1920

1925

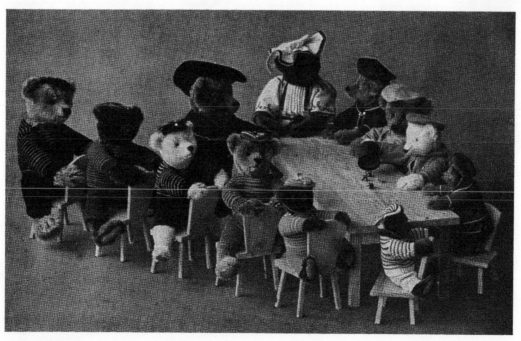

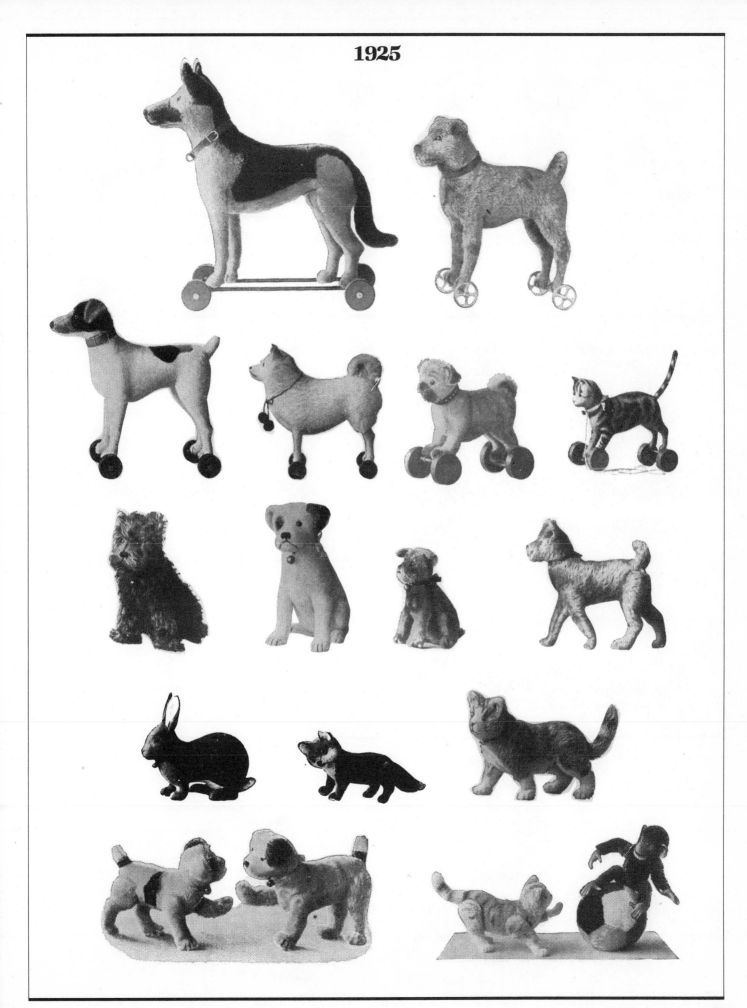

1925

1925

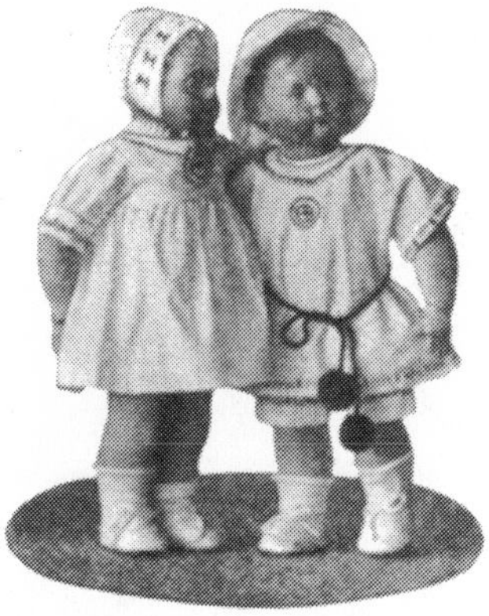
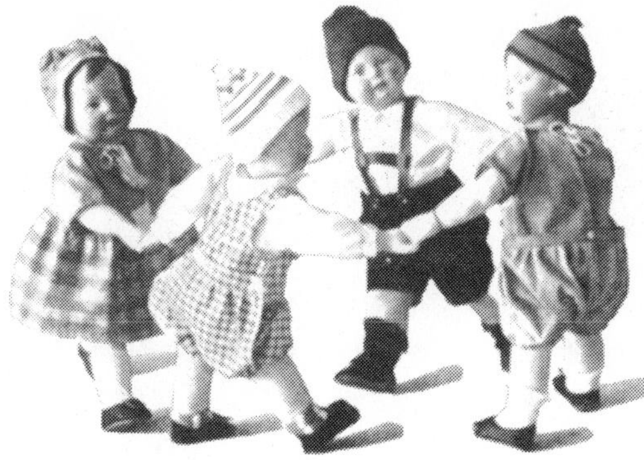
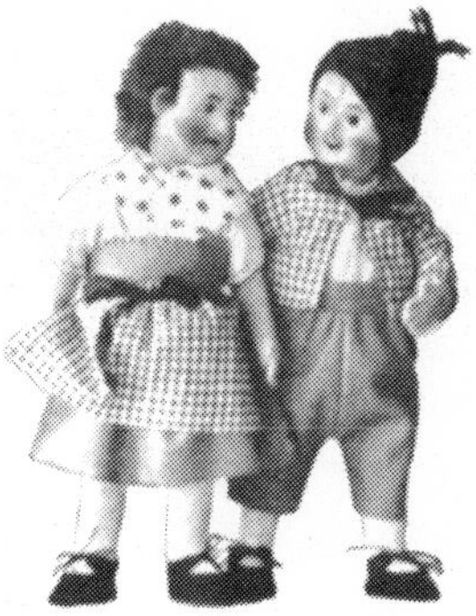
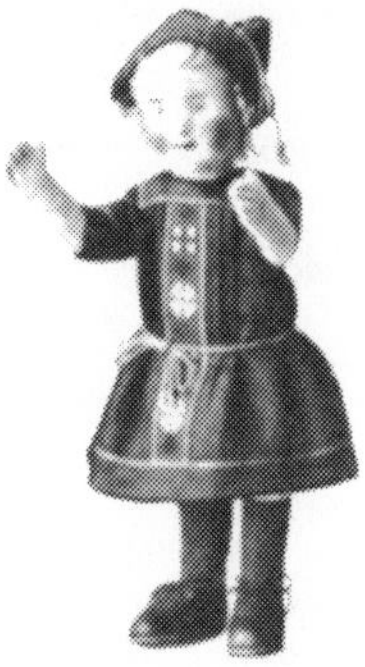
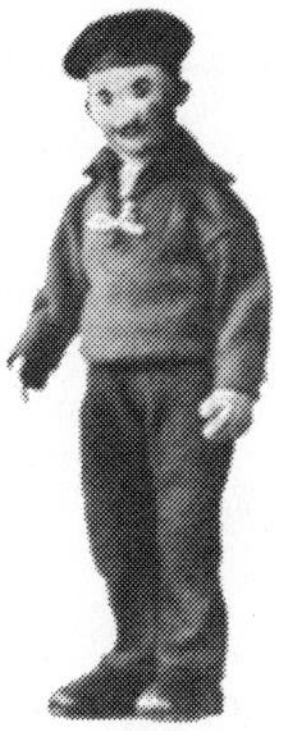
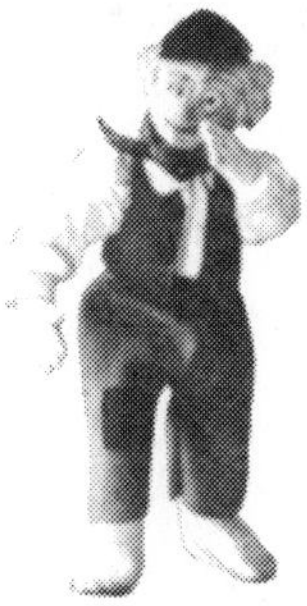
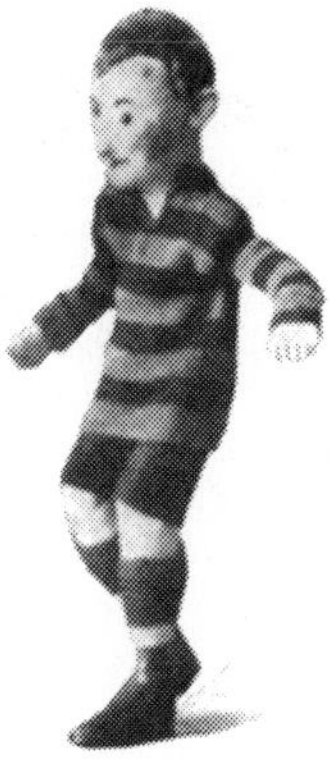
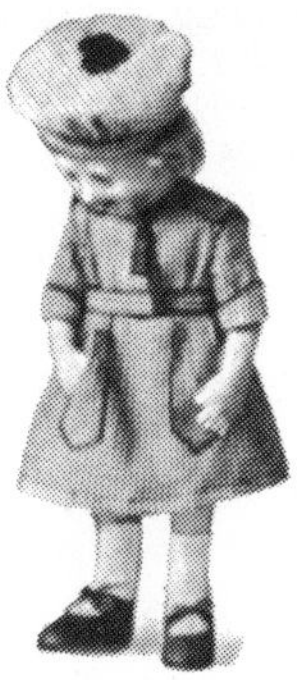
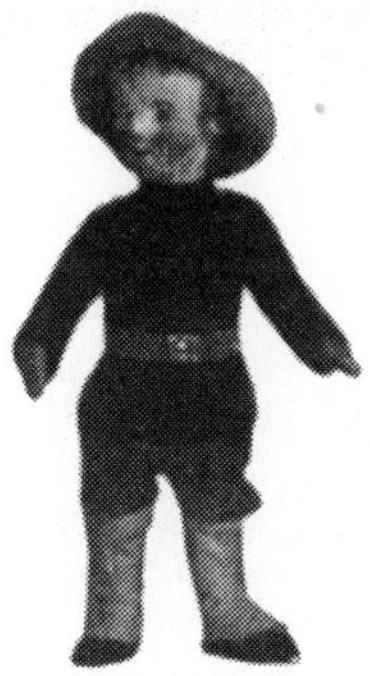
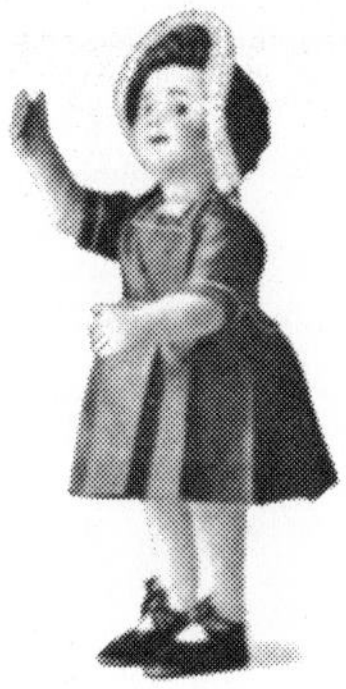
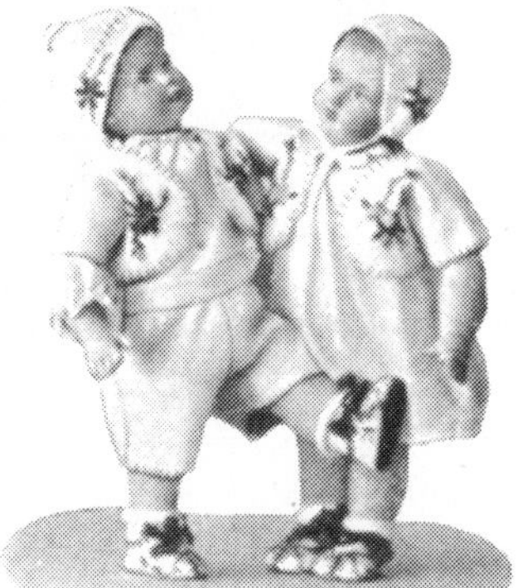
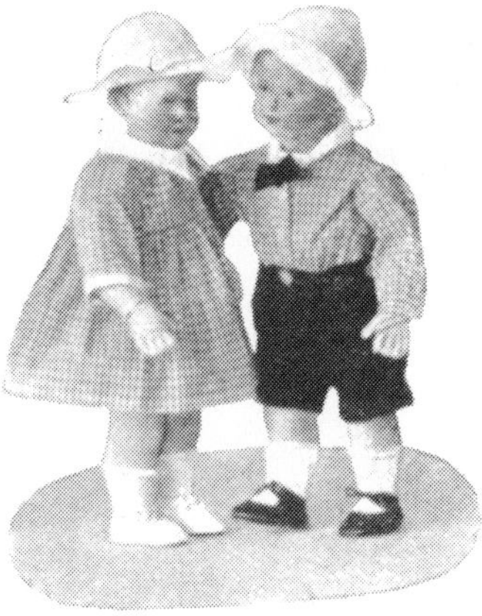
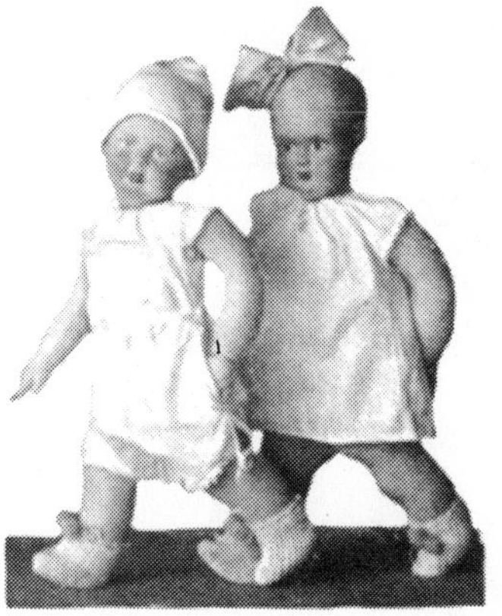
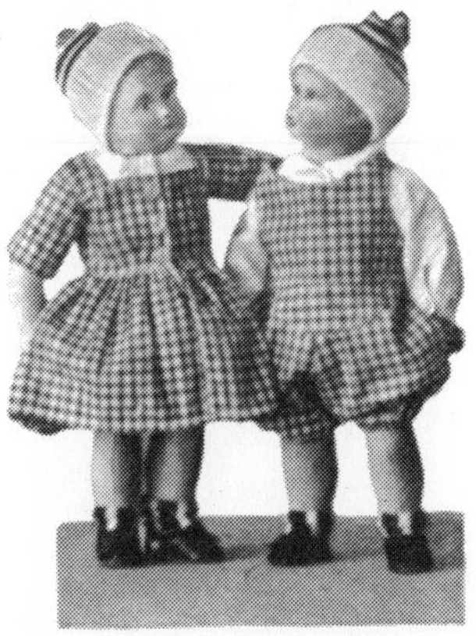
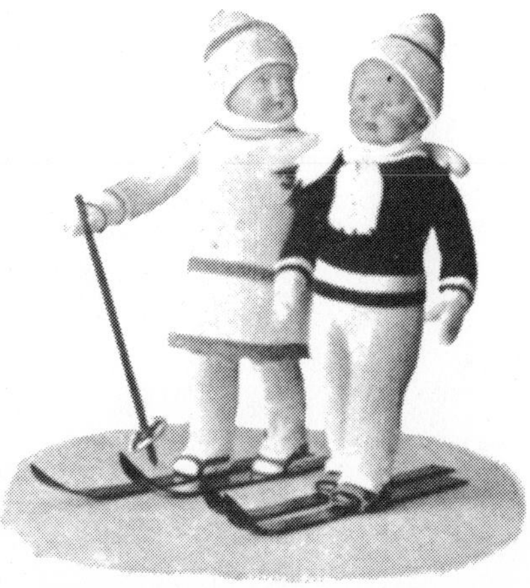
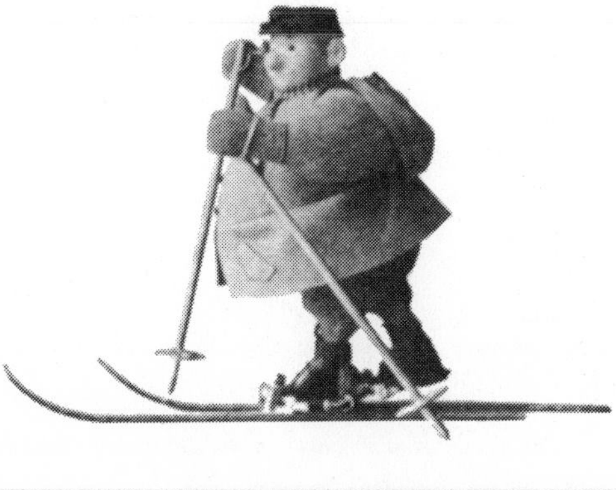

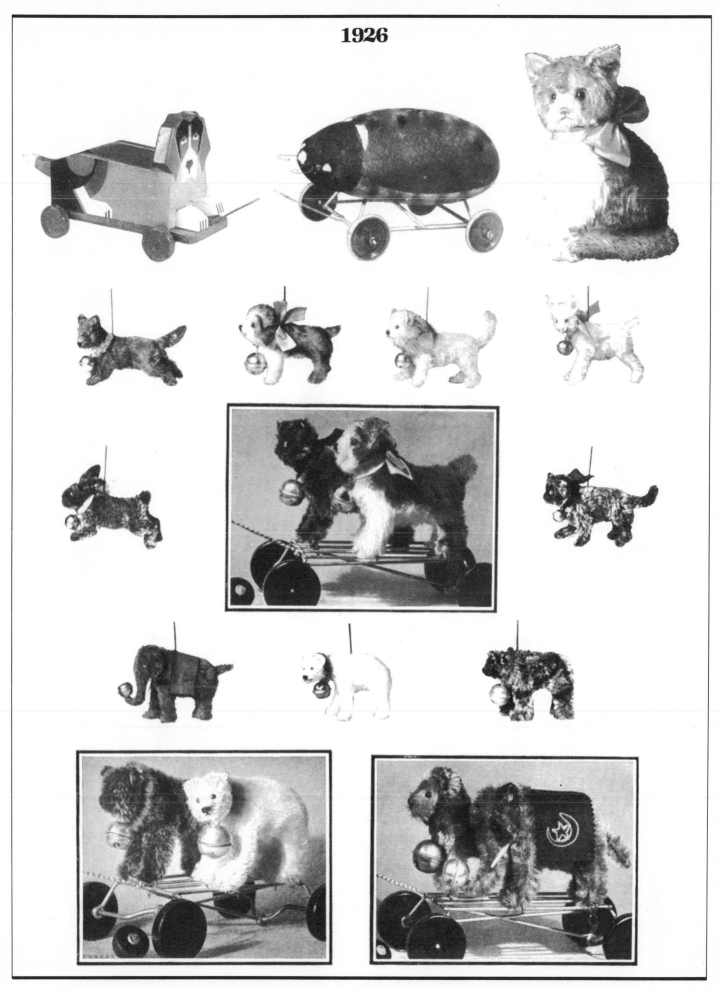

1928

1932

1938

1939-1940

1948

1951-1952

1951-1952

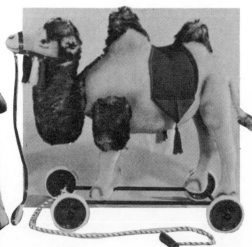

Old bears in museum under photograph of Richard Steiff.

Richard Steiff's first bear.

Margaret Strong Bears, 1982.

Window depicting various trademarks.

Large display animals in Steiff showroom.

This bowling set goes back to earliest catalogs.

Elephants, old and new.

Sailor doll with pressed-felt face.

Unusual Schlopsnies doll with celluloid head.

Assortment of rabbits from museum.

Assortment of miniatures from the 1950s.

Window in Steiff Museum showing earliest Steiff dolls.

Peasant couple from before World War I.

Elegant doll couple from museum.

Musician dolls from before World War I.

Clown doll.

Gucki Dwarf, loaned by Wolf Toy Store, Giengen.

Rudi and Else dolls from the 1930s (pressed-felt faces).

Wooden games and puzzles.

Gnomes from the 1930s.

Rocking horse on wheels, loaned by Herr Hohnold.

Wooden cart pulled by felt rabbits.

Horse and cart from the 1950s.

Wooden vehicles made by Steiff.

Steiff Dolls, Teddy Bears, and Toys with Prices

Keeping close tabs on current prices for Steiff toys and dolls is not an easy task, but by watching ads in trade papers, attending antique shows and sales, and through contact with collectors, it is possible to provide a range of prices people are paying for these antiques and collectibles.

Prices are always relative and vary according to the desire of the purchaser for a particular item. Many of the items pictured are in the Steiff Museum in Giengen, Germany. Some are so rare as to defy pricing. Examples from the museum are indicated with the letter *M* in parentheses.

The dolls in particular are very unusual, and they are priced in relation to their sizes and accessories. Condition and rarity are the main factors to consider in individual cases. Prices at the highest levels are for specimens in the best condition.

A bit of advice: Pay what seems right to you for these or any other collectible.

Woman, 15″, felt body, jointed, glass eyes, mohair wig, cotton dress, underwear, leather belt and shoes, before 1914 (M), **$450-550.**

Dolls and Animals Dressed as Dolls

Students, 16″, felt bodies, jointed, glass eyes, mohair wigs, leather shoes, felt clothes, before 1914 (M), **$550-650 each.**

Man, 18″, felt body, jointed, glass eyes, mohair wig, felt clothes, wooden shoes, before 1914 (M), **$650-750.**

Tall Man, 23″, felt body, jointed, glass eyes, mohair wig, felt suit, cotton shirt, hat, embroidered vest with brass buttons, leather boots, before 1914 (M), **$850-950.**

Peasant Couple, 19½″, felt bodies, jointed, glass eyes, mohair wigs, cotton clothes, leather boots, tin button on lady's scarf, before 1914 (M), **$650-750 each.**

Waiter, 13″, felt body, jointed, glass eyes, mohair wig, mustache, cotton clothes, felt shoes, before 1914, **$350-450.**

Schwabian Farmer (left), 23″, felt body, jointed, glass eyes, mohair wig, cotton clothes, leather boots, felt hat, pipe, and whip, before 1914 (M), **$850-950.** Infantry Grenadier (right), 21″, felt body, jointed, glass eyes, mohair wig, felt clothes, leather belt and boots, brass buttons on costume, brass sword, before 1914 (M), **$750-850.**

Swiss Soldier, 6″, felt body, jointed, glass eyes, mohair wig, felt clothes, leather shoes, belt with sword and buckle, before 1914, **$150-250.**

Boy, 7″, felt body, jointed, glass eyes, mohair wig, felt clothes, felt hat with tassel, before 1914, **$150-250.**

Girl, 11″, felt body, jointed, glass eyes, mohair wig, cotton dress, knit socks, shoes missing, before 1914, **$250-350.**

Soldier, 9″, felt body, jointed, glass eyes, mohair wig, felt uniform, brass buttons, tricolored ribbon, leather shoes, felt spats, before 1914, **$200-300.**

Lady, 12″, felt body, jointed, glass eyes, mohair wig, cotton clothes with velvet trim, cotton scarf, umbrella not original, leather shoes, before 1914, **$350-450.**

Girl, 16″, felt body, jointed, glass eyes, mohair wig, felt clothes, cotton blouse, felt shoes, before 1914, **$550-650.**

Dutch and Tyrolean Girls, 12″, felt bodies, jointed, glass eyes, mohair wigs, cotton clothes, felt hats and shoes, tin button, before 1914, **$350-450** each.

Musician, 15″, felt body, jointed, glass eyes, mohair wig, felt jacket with brass buttons, cotton trousers, leather belt with ax and rope, boots with Steiff buttons, brass helmet with red plume, brass cymbal and drum, before 1914 (M), **$650-750.**

Musician, 16″, felt body, jointed, glass eyes, mohair wig, felt clothes, leather shoes, wooden base, brass trumpet, before 1914 (M), **$550-650.**

Boy, 16″, felt body, jointed, glass eyes, mohair wig, felt pants, jacket, vest, hat, brass buttons, leather boots, before 1914 (M), **$550-650.**
Ladies, 16″, felt bodies, jointed, glass eyes, mohair wigs, cotton clothes, before 1914 (M), **$550-650** each.

Musician, 11″, felt body, jointed, glass eyes, mohair wig, felt clothes with Steiff buttons on front, leather shoes, wooden base with bass fiddle, before 1914 (M), **$450-550.**

Boy, 9″, felt body, jointed, glass eyes, mohair wig, felt pants, straw hat, cane, carrying prayer book, before 1914, **$200-250.**

Girl, 9″, felt body, jointed, glass eyes, mohair wig, felt vest with brass buttons, carrying prayer book, before 1914, **$200-250.**

School Girl, 11″, felt body, jointed, glass eyes, mohair wig, mohair-lined school bag, writing slate, before 1914, **$300-400.**

Sharkey (left), 15″, felt, jointed, glass eyes, mohair wig, felt uniform, spats, leather shoes, backpack, canteen, satchel, leather straps and belt, felt hat with rope, brass buttons, before 1914 (M), **$550-650.** Tommy (right), 17″, felt, jointed, glass eyes, mohair wig, felt uniform, leather shoes and belt, felt hat, **$550-650.**

Man, 15″, felt body, jointed, button eyes, felt clothes, leather shoes, squeaker in hat, 1908, **$450-550.**

Indian, 16″, felt body, jointed, glass eyes, mohair wig, felt vest and pants, cotton shirt, knit tie, leather moccasins, before 1914, **$550-650.**

Man, 16″, felt body, jointed, glass eyes, mohair wig, felt and cotton clothes, top hat, leather shoes, before 1914, **$450-550.**

Man, 20″, felt body, jointed, glass eyes, mohair wig, felt and cotton clothes, leather boots, top hat, **$650-750.** Lady, 18″, felt and silk clothing, before 1914 (M), **$650-750.**

Clownie, 17″, felt body, jointed, rubber head, mohair wig, cotton clothes, 1950s, **$200-250.**

Santa Claus, 14″ felt with rubber head, jointed, mohair beard, felt clothes, 1950s (M), **$200-250.**
Santa Claus, 5″, **$75-125.**

Santa Claus, 11½″, felt body, **$150-200.**

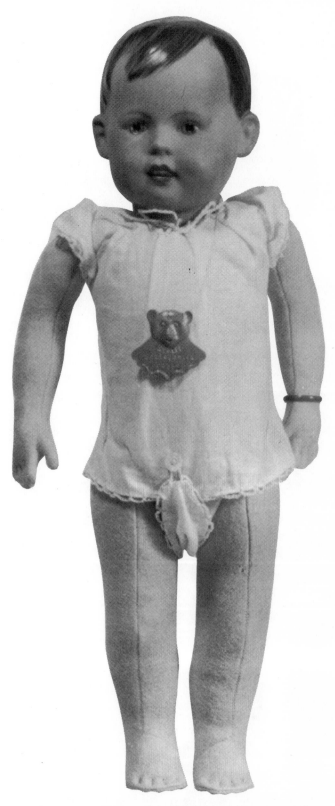

Schlopsnies Child, 16″, celluloid head painted from inside, felt body with sewn arms, jointed legs, painted eyes, cotton clothes, blue plastic tag on neck, red plastic bracelet on arm, 1922 (M), **$850-950.**

Cowboy, 8″, felt body, rubber head, felt and cotton clothes, 1950s, **$100-150.**

Uwe, 15″, flat-faced felt, plastic eyes, synthetic clothes, 1960, **$25-50.**

Boy Mechanic, 14″, pressed-felt face, jointed body, glass eyes, mohair wig, cotton clothes, leather belt (M), **$450-550.** Rita, 14″, tin button on arm band, 1930-1952 (M), **$450-550.**

Bunny, 16″, mohair, glass eyes, sewn nose and mouth, velvet clothes sewn on body, leather shoes, early, **$350-450.**

Ski Bunny, 16″, mohair, glass eyes, sewn nose and mouth, jointed head and arms, ski pole, 1960s (M), **$100-150.**

Elf, 10″, felt body, mohair beard, glass eyes, removable mushroom hat, 1930s (M), **$100-150.**

Elf, 7″, felt with hat, mohair beard, side-glancing eyes, removable felt shoes, tin button, 1934, **$75-125.**

Coffee Cosies, felt heads, felt jointed arms, cotton and felt clothes, 1905-1914 (M), **$250-350** each.

Animal Dolls, 10″, rayon plush, glass eyes, felt mouths, cotton clothes, World War II (M), **$100-150** each.

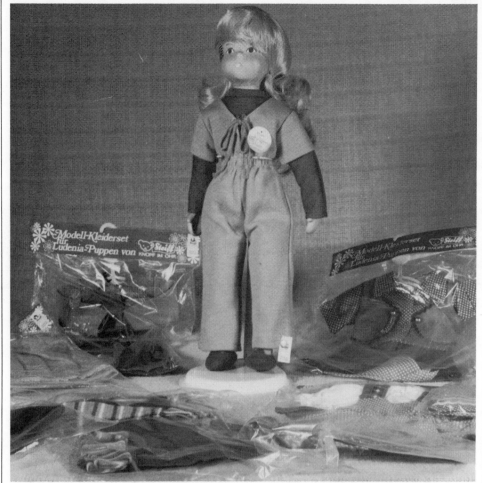

Steffi, 14″, soft cloth body, plastic face, painted eyes, blond wig, seven outfits, 1970s, **$50-75.**

Mecki Family. Mecki (left), 6½″, jointed, felt body, rubber head, cotton and felt clothes, leather shoes, 1950s, **$75-125.** Mucki (center), 4½″, **$25-50.** Micki (right), 6½″, **$75-125.**

Mickey Mouse, 12″, felt body, painted eyes, velvet clothes, removable shoes, 1930s, **$350-450.**

Pig, 10″, pink mohair, glass eyes, velvet hands and mouth, jointed, felt jacket, linen hat, 1930s, **$150-200.**

Grasshopper, 18″, mohair, felt clothes, plastic antennae, glass eyes, 1950s, **$100-150.**

Animals Dressed as Dolls (continued)

Waldi, 11″, mohair, glass eyes, jointed, felt clothes, gun, 1938, **$150-200.**

Monkey, 8″, mohair, jointed, glass eyes, felt clothes, 1953, **$100-150.**

Mouse, 8″, velvet, jointed, button eyes, nose, felt clothes, 1953, **$100-150.**

Teddy Bears

Teddy B by Steiff.

Teddy Bear (left), 20″, dark red mohair, jointed, sewn nose and mouth, button eyes, felt pads, rare, tag on ear, **$800-1,000.** Bear (right), 16″, light red mohair, jointed, same description, **$600-800.**

Teddy Bear, 22″, blond mohair, jointed, sewn nose and mouth, button eyes, felt pads, hump, long arms (M), 1908, **$1,000-1,500.**

Teddy Bear, 8″, tan mohair, jointed, sewn nose and mouth, button eyes, felt pads, 1930s, **$200-300.** Bear, 30″, white mohair, early, **$1,000-1,500.**

Teddy Bear, 20″, gold mohair, jointed, sewn nose and mouth, glass eyes, felt pads, long arms, blue satin ribbon, chrome button (M), **$800-1,000.**

Teddy Bear (left), 16½″, gold mohair, jointed, sewn nose and mouth, button eyes, tin button, **$600-800.** Teddy (right), 17″, gold mohair, **$600-800.**

Teddy Bear, 15″, blond mohair, jointed, sewn nose and mouth, button eyes, replaced leather pads, hump, long arms (M), 1908, **$400-600.**

Standing Bear, 8", plush on wooden frame with brushes, early elephant tag, button eyes (M), 1898, **$400-500.**

Teddy Bear, 13½", honey mohair, jointed, sewn nose and mouth, glass eyes, felt pads, hump, long arms (M), **$400-600.**

Teddy Bear, 16", pink mohair, jointed, sewn nose and mouth, glass eyes, hump, felt pads, long arms, tin button, rare (M), **$800-1,000.**

Standing Bear (left), 8", wooden rolypoly with burlap-type covering, button eyes, 1898 (M), **$400-500.** Metal die of early elephant trademark (center). Standing Bear (right) described earlier.

Teddy Bears, 10", white, brown, and honey mohair, jointed, sewn nose and mouth, button eyes, humps, felt pads, long arms, tags, tin buttons, 1913 (M), **$300-400** each.

Teddy Bear, 13″, honey mohair, jointed, sewn nose and mouth, button eyes, felt pads, long arms, tin button (M), **$400-600.**

Bear, 8″, brown rough plush, sewn nose and mouth, button eyes, felt pads, metal wheels (M), 1914, **$300-400.**

Creeping Bear, 7½″ x 16″, brown mohair, sewn nose and mouth, glass eyes, hump, felt pads, 1934 (M), **$200-300.**

Bear, 11½″, brennessel fabric, sewn nose and mouth, button eyes, leather collar, hump, metal wheels, tin button, rare, 1914 (M), **$400-500.**

Teddy Bear, 12″, tan mohair, jointed, sewn nose and mouth, button eyes, felt pads (M), **$300-400.**

Standing Bear, 13″, honey mohair, jointed, sewn nose and mouth, glass eyes, felt pads, hump (M), **$400-600.** Sitting Bear, 10½″, yellow mohair (M), **$300-400.**

Teddy Bear, 8″, golden mohair, jointed, sewn nose and mouth, glass eyes, felt pads, hump, dressed in hunting clothes (M), 1953, **$150-200.**

Teddy on Wheels, 9″, brown mohair, jointed, sewn mouth and nose, button eyes, wooden wheels, 1950s (M), **$200-250.**

Teddy Baby (left), 11″, brown mohair, jointed, sewn nose and mouth, glass eyes, felt feet and mouth, leather collar, 1930 (M), **$250-350.** Large Teddy Baby (center), 17″ blond mohair, **$400-600.** Teddy Baby (right), 16½″, blond mohair, **$400-600.**

Teddy Bears, mohair, jointed, sewn nose and mouth, button eyes. Smallest bear is not a Steiff. Bears, 5½″, **$200-250.** Bears, 3½″, **$100-150.**

Teddy Bear, 6″, gold mohair, jointed, sewn nose and mouth, glass eyes, pink ribbon, **$150-200.**

Teddy Bear Rattle, 5½″, buff mohair, jointed, sewn nose and mouth, button eyes, rattle inside, tin button, **$250-300.**

Basket of Bears. Bears, 3½″ mohair, jointed, sewn mouth and nose, button eyes, 1950s, **$100-150.** Bear, 8″, mohair, **$200-300.** Bear, 6″, white mohair, new.

Standing Bear, 7″ x 7½″, brown, 80 percent Dralon, 20 percent cotton, red ribbon, felt mouth and pads, glass eyes, chrome button, 1950s, **$50-75.**

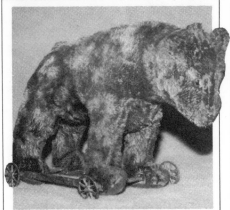

Bear on Wheels, 8″ x 10½″, brown mohair, sewn nose and mouth, button eyes, metal wheels, 1910, **$500-600.**

Polar Bear, 20″, white mohair, jointed legs, sewn nose and mouth, swivel neck, button eyes (M), **$500-600.**

Bear Muff, white mohair, sewn nose and mouth, glass eyes, ribbon, felt pads, 1960s, **$50-75.**

Panda Bear, 8½″, black and white mohair, jointed, felt mouth, 1950s, **$100-150.** Panda, 2½″, wool and cotton, **$15-25.**

Koala Bear, 8½″, tan, long and short mohair, jointed, sewn nose and mouth, glass eyes, 1950s, **$100-150.**

Zotty Bear, 20", tan curly mohair, jointed, sewn nose, felt mouth, glass eyes, 1950s, **$300-400.**

Teddy Bear, 17", honey mohair, jointed, sewn nose and mouth, glass eyes, 1969, **$100-150.**

Teddy Bear, 14", brown mohair, jointed, sewn nose and mouth, glass eyes, felt pads, 1966 (M), **$100-150.**

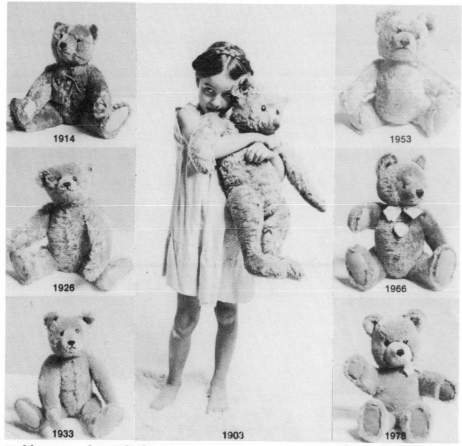

1914

1953

1926

1966

1933

1903

1978

Teddy Bears through the years.

Teddy Bear, 22", caramel, jointed, sewn nose and mouth, glass eyes, felt pads, 1958, **$500-600.**

Teddy Bear Tea Party. Four 6″ mohair bears in assorted colors, china tea set on plastic table with cloth, 1982, **$175** set.

Assorted White Bears, five different sizes, 1982, **$275** set.

Animals

Centennial Bear, 16″, gold mohair, jointed, sewn nose and mouth, button eyes, 1980, **$400-500.**

Dog on Wheels, 19½″ x 20″, mohair with steel frame, felt mouth and ears, eyes missing, pull squeaker, worn, "U.S. Zone Germany" tag, **$200-250.**

Margaret Strong Bears. Large Bear, 13″, caramel mohair, jointed, button eyes, curved arms, hump, 1982, **$75.** Small Bear, 9″, **$45.**

Mama, 14″, and Baby, 6″, 1981, **$150-200** set.

Poodles, 4″, long and short mohair, jointed, glass eyes, **$25-50** each.

Monkey, 11″, 5″ tail, white mohair, jointed, felt face, hands and feet, green glass eyes, no eyelids, seamed face, tin button, early, **$200-300.**

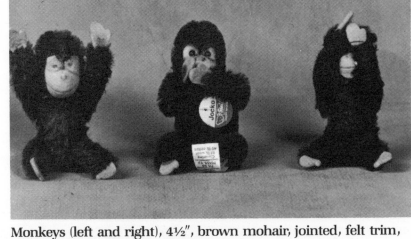

Monkeys (left and right), 4½″, brown mohair, jointed, felt trim, 1950s, **$50-75.** Middle monkey is new.

Monkey, 6½″, white mohair, jointed, felt face and ears, 1950s, **$75-125.**

Orangutans, orange mohair, jointed, glass eyes, cardboard tags, tin buttons, 1930; 7″, **$150-200;** 6″, **$125-175;** 5″, **$100-150;** 4″, **$75-125.**

Baboon, 4″, gray mohair, jointed, felt trim, red collar and behind, 1950s, **$50-75.**

Monkey, 6½″ brown felt, wooden wheels, 1912 (M), **$200-300.**

Bison, 10″, brown mohair and felt, glass eyes, metal wheels, pull toy (M), 1914, **$400-500.**

Monkey (left), 14″, brown mohair, jointed, brown felt face, paws and feet, tin button, 1908 (M), **$300-400.** Monkey (right), 12″, **$200-300.**

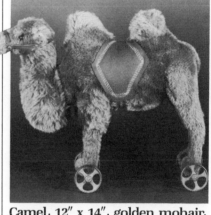

Camel, 12″ x 14″, golden mohair, button eyes, metal wheels, early, **$400-500.**

Monkey (left), 10″, brown mohair, jointed, felt face, hands and paws, 1925 (M), **$200-250.** Radiator Cap (left center), 10″, brown mohair, 1913, rare (M), **$300-400.** Monkey (right center), 8″, 1925, **$150-200.** Monkey (right), 7″, **$100-150.**

Camel, 11″, golden mohair, button eyes, early, **$400-500.**

Camel, 5½″, tan mohair, felt ears, velvet legs and face, 1950s, **$50-75.**

Hippos, 2½″ gray mohair, felt ears, mouth, and feet pads, 1950s, **$50-75** each.

Tiger Cubs, orange and black mohair, glass eyes. Tiger (left), 4″, jointed head, **$25-50.** Tiger (right), 3½″ x 6″, **$25-50.**

Zebra, 10″, rough plush, gray and white, button eyes, wheels missing, tin button (M), before World War I, **$250-350.**

Zebra (left), 8″, black and white mohair, long mohair on tail and mane, 1950s, **$75-100.** Zebra (right), 5″, felt, **$50-75.**

Lion, 12″ x 13″, yellow mohair, glass eyes, metal wheels, early, **$400-500.**

Lion, 4½″, cream and brown mohair, glass eyes, mohair mane and tip of tail, 1950s, **$50-75.**

Lion Cub, 4″, gold mohair, jointed, glass eyes, 1950s, **$50-75.**

Giraffe, 7″, gold and orange velvet, felt ears, glass eyes, 1950s, **$25-50.**

Ocelot, 6½″ x 13″, gold and black mohair, sewn nose and mouth, 1955, **$100-150.**

Giraffe, 11″, gold and orange mohair, felt ears, glass eyes, 1950s, **$75-100.**

Reindeer, 9″, tan mohair, felt antlers, glass eyes, sewn nose and mouth, 1950s, **$100-150.**

Reindeer, 12½″, tan mohair, felt antlers, glass eyes, sewn nose and mouth, **$150-200.**

Mountain Goat, 5″ x 6″, gray mohair, felt horns, glass eyes, chrome button, 1950s, **$50-75.**

Goat, 5″, white mohair, black velvet legs, glass eyes, **$50-75.**

Fox, 7″ x 10″ (not including tail), reddish-brown mohair, jointed, glass eyes, 1925, **$250-300.**

Moles, 4″, black mohair, glass eyes, felt noses, plastic shovels, **$25-50.**

Hamster, 5″, gold mohair, jointed head, glass eyes, felt paws and mouth, **$50-75.**

Porcupines, brown mohair, felt ears and feet, jointed head, **$50-75** each.

Badger, 6½″, black and white mohair, glass eyes, felt paws, **$50-75.**

Mice (left and center), 3″, gray mohair, felt paws and ears, **$25-50.** Mouse (right), 2″, white mohair, **$25-50.** Mouse (front), mini wool, **$15-25.**

Kangaroo, 11″, tan mohair, jointed, open pouch with plastic baby, glass eyes, **$150-200.**

Squirrel, 3½", brown, long and short mohair, glass eyes, felt paws, **$50-75.**

Squirrel, 7", gold, long and short mohair, glass eyes, velvet nut, **$75-100.**

Raccoon, 8½", gray Dralon, sewn nose and mouth, glass eyes, felt paws, **$25-50.**

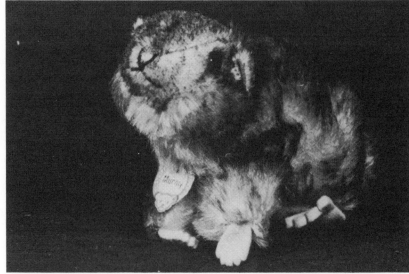

Groundhog, 6", brown mohair, felt paws, glass eyes, sewn nose, **$50-75.**

Beaver (center), 5", brown mohair, felt paws, tail, and mouth. **$50-75.** Beavers (left and right), 3½", **$25-50.**

Skunk (left), 4", black and white mohair, sewn nose and mouth, glass eyes, felt paws, **$50-100.** Skunk (right), 2½", wool mini, **$15-25.**

Duck, 10″, multi-felt, velvet, glass eyes, metal wheels, 1898 (M), **$500-600.**

Stork, 24″, white and black felt, glass eyes, metal legs covered with felt, 1898 (M), **$500-600.** Swan, 13½″, white and black felt and velvet, glass eyes, metal wheels, 1898 (M), **$300-400.** Swan, 4″ (M), **$150-200.**

Goose, 16″, white mohair, button eyes, jointed metal legs covered with felt (M), **$300-400.** Goose, 10″, **$200-300.**

Rooster, 7½″, multi-felt, glass eyes, metal legs covered with felt, 1898 (M), **$250-350.**

Rooster, 14″, multi-felt, metal eyes, metal legs covered with felt, 1898 (M), **$500-600.**

Hen, 14″, multi-mohair, glass eyes, felt trim, jointed legs, early (M), **$400-500.**

Hen, 6″, multi-mohair, button eyes, felt feet, comb and tail, chrome button, 1950s, **$50-75.**

Rooster, 12″, multi-mohair, glass eyes, felt feet, comb, and tail, metal legs covered with felt, **$200-250.** Hen, 7″, felt beak, **$50-75.**

Rooster, 14″, multi-felt, button eyes, metal legs covered with felt, 1898 (M), **$500-600.**

Large Owl, 9½", multi-mohair, glass eyes, felt trim, metal legs covered with felt, **$100-150.** Small Owl, 4", **$50-75.**

Pelican, 6½", white mohair, felt and vinyl beak, felt feet, metal legs covered with felt, **$50-75.**

Duck, 5", multi-mohair, glass eyes, felt beak, jointed neck, 1930s (M), **$75-125.**

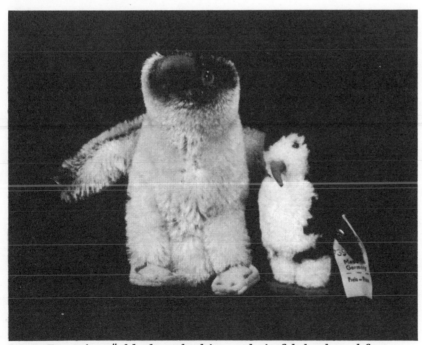

Large Penguin, 4", black and white mohair, felt beak and feet, glass eyes, **$50-75.** Small Penguin, 2½", wool and felt mini, **$15-25.**

Parrot, 10", multi-mohair, glass eyes, metal feet covered with felt, **$100-150.**

Crow, 7″, black mohair, glass eyes, felt beak, tail, and wings, metal legs, **$50-75.**

Bat, 4½″, 8″ wingspan, gray mohair body, felt ears, plastic wings, chrome button, 1950s, **$150-200.**

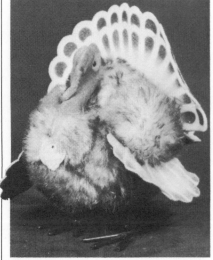

Turkey, 5½″, long mohair body, felt wings and tail, velvet head, metal legs and feet, **$50-75.**

Alligator, 29″, multi-mohair, glass eyes, felt mouth and fins, 1952 (M), **$150-200.** Brontosaurus, 15″, gray multi-mohair, glass eyes, 1960 (M), **$100-150.** Dinosaur, 14″, multi-mohair, glass eyes, felt fins, 1960 (M), **$100-150.** Lizard, 10″, multi-felt, glass eyes, 1959 (M), **$50-75.**

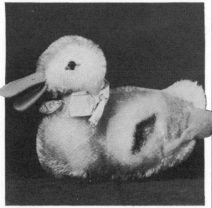

Duck, 4″, multi-mohair, felt beak and feet, **$50-75.**

Birds, wool minis, felt trim, wire legs, **$15-25** each.

Turtle, 5″, mohair, vinyl shell, glass eyes, **$50-75.**

Large Fish, 11″, multi-mohair, glass eyes, felt lips and mouth, **$50-75.** Small Fish, 5″, **$25-50.**

Snail, 6½″, multi-velvet, vinyl shell, rubber antennae, **$50-75.**

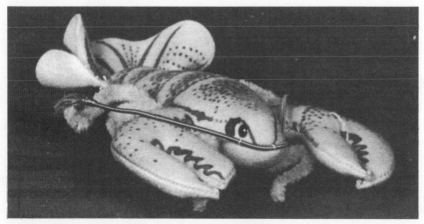

Lobster, 7″, orange felt, glass eyes, **$50-75.**

Large Frog, 7″ x 12″, green multi-mohair, glass eyes, **$150-200.** Small Frog, 3″ x 4″, felt, **$50-75.**

Large Seal, 6½″, gray mohair, glass eyes, sewn nose and mouth, felt ears, **$75-100.** Small Seal, 5″, **$50-75.**

Pony, 5½″, white and brown mohair, felt ears, vinyl saddle and bridle, **$50-75.**

Pony, 6½″, black and white mohair, long mohair mane and tail, felt ears, **$75-100.**

Horse, 10″, tan felt, horsehair mane and tail, glass eyes, wooden wheels, tin button, leather saddle, pull toy (M), **$300-400.**

Large Donkey, 24″, gray felt, leather saddle, button eyes, metal wheels, 1900 (M), **$500-600.** Small Donkey, 10″, wooden wheels, 1929 (M), **$300-400.**

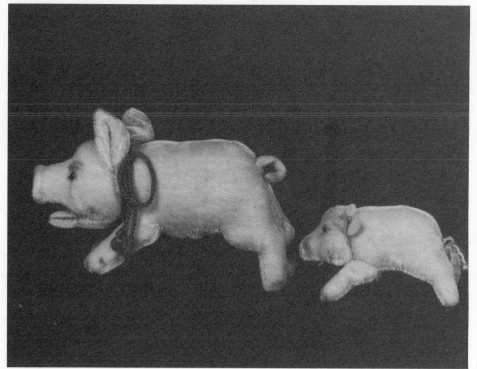

Large Pig, 6½″, pink mohair, felt mouth and tail, cord on neck, $100-150. Small Pig, 4″, $50-75.

Lamb, 14″, white mohair, glass eyes, sewn nose and mouth, ribbon and bell, $150-200.

Cow, 6″, multi-mohair, felt horns, leather collar and bell, felt udders and mouth, $75-125.

Pig, 3″, pink felt, button eyes, tin button, 1925 (M), $100-150.

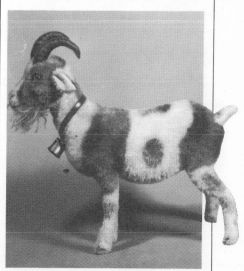

Goat, 13″, multi-mohair, glass eyes, felt horns, leather collar and bell, 1938 (M), $250-300.

Rabbit, 15″, tan mohair, glass eyes, felt mouth (M), **$150-200.**

Novelties (M). Hide-a-Gift mohair heads, felt bottoms, glass eyes, **$50-75.** Chicken Hat, 1913, **$150-200.** Egg Warmers, 1913, **$75-125.**

Rabbit, 16″, tan mohair, glass eyes, jointed, 1952, **$150-200.**

Rabbit, 16″, tan mohair, glass eyes, jointed, 1974, **$75-125.**

Hand Puppets, 10″, mohair, glass eyes, 1927-1930 (M), **$75-100.**

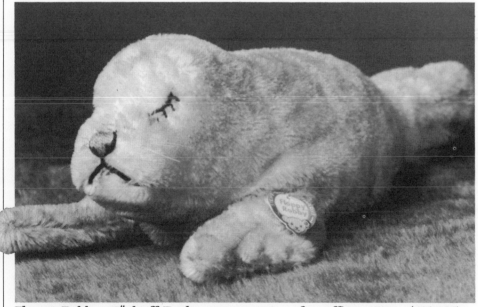

Floppy Animals, 5½″, mohair, sewn eyes, soft stuffing, 1950s, **$50-75** each.

Floppy Robby, 12″, buff Dralon, sewn eyes, soft stuffing, 1950s, **$75-125**.

Siamese Cat, 8″, tan mohair, glass eyes, jointed head, red ribbon on neck, 1953 (M), **$75-125**.

Cat, 5″, black velvet body, mohair tail, sewn nose and mouth, glass eyes, ribbon on neck, 1960s, **$50-75**.

Cat, 4″, gray and white mohair, glass eyes, sewn nose and mouth, **$50-75**.

Cat, 6½″, gray and white mohair, jointed head, glass eyes, sewn nose and mouth, ribbon and bell, **$75-125.**

Dog, 6½″, long mohair, glass eyes, collar and bell, wooden wheels with hopping action, 1929, **$200-250.** Cat, 6½″, gray and white felt, glass eyes, ribbon, wooden wheels with hopping action, pull toy, 1932 (M), **$200-250.**

Rattler, 10½″, gray mohair, glass eyes, red collar, tail moves head in swivel motion, tin button, 1932, **$150-200.**

Cat, 3″, black and white velvet, glass eyes, ribbon and bell, 1927, **$75-125.** Large Dog, 6″, black and white mohair, collar and bell, 1927, **$150-200.** Small Dog, 4″ (M), **$100-150.**

Zeppelin Mascot, 11″, light brown, long and short mohair, glass eyes, sewn nose and mouth, 1928, **$150-200.**

Bonzo Dogs, printed velvet, tin buttons, glass eyes, 1930. Dog (left), 8″, jointed, **$150-200.** Dog (center), 10″, jointed head, **$200-250.** Dog (right), 13½″, jointed, **$250-300.**

Dachshund, 24″, brown felt, glass eyes, leather collar, wooden wheels, pull toy, 1914 (M), **$400-500.**

Bulldog, 8″ x 10″, brown plush, jointed, glass eyes, sewn nose and mouth, original collar and leash, 1908, **$250-300.**

Dog, 7″, tan felt, glass eyes, sewn nose and mouth, 1913, **$250-300.**

Dog, 13½″, gold and brown mohair, glass eyes, metal wheels, 1913, **$400-500.**

Terrier, 6″ x 8″, long mohair, cream, black, tan, 1950s, **$50-75.**

Laika, the dog that traveled into space, 6½″, white, long and short mohair, sewn nose and mouth, **$100-150.**

Dachshund (left), **12″**, brown felt, tin button, leather collar with bell, button eyes, 1916, **$300-400.** Dachshund (right), **12″**, velvet, button eyes, leather collar and bell, 1914 (M), **$300-400.**

Spaniel, 4½″, black and white mohair, glass eyes, **$50-75.**

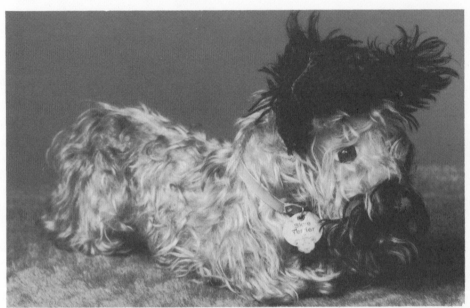

Skye Terrier, 13″, gray and black curly mohair, glass eyes, red collar, tin button, 1932, **$100-150.**

Schnauzer, 10″, Dralon, felt ears, sewn nose and mouth, **$50-75.**

Spaniels, mohair, jointed head, felt mouth. Large Dog, 6″, **$75-125.** Small Dogs, 4″, **$50-75.**

Basset Hound, 9″ mohair with velvet nose, glass eyes, $75-125.

Schnauzers, gray mohair, glass eyes, swivel neck, sewn nose and mouth, leather collar, 1931 (M). Left, 9″, **$150-200.** Center, 5″, **$75-125.** Right, 13½″, **$200-250.**

Dalmatian, 6½″, mohair, felt mouth, sewn nose, leather collar, jointed head, **$50-75.**

Cocker Spaniels, long and short mohair, jointed head, sewn nose, felt mouth. Large Dog, 6½″, **$75-125.** Small Dogs, 3½″, **$50-75.**

Terriers, mohair, glass eyes, collar, red saddle (left), 3″, **$40-60.** Terrier (center), 4″, **$50-75.** Terrier (right), 2½″, **$25-50.**

Pug, 9″, short and long mohair, felt tongue, jointed head, sewn nose, **$75-125.**

German Shepherd, 9½", long and short mohair, felt mouth and tongue, leather collar, sewn nose, **$75-125.**

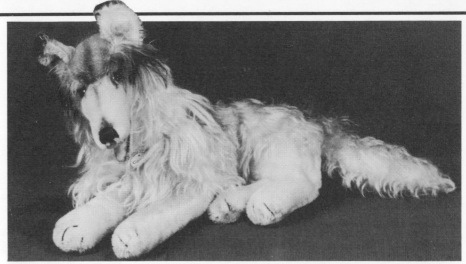

Collie, 20½" x 10", long and short mohair, felt mouth, sewn nose, glass eyes, **$150-200.**

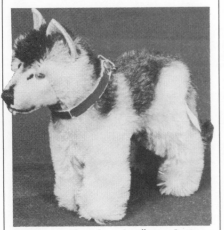

German Shepherd, 4", mohair, felt face and ears, sewn nose, plastic collar, **$50-75.**

Dachshunds, mohair, jointed head, leather collar, glass eyes, sewn nose and mouth. Large Dog, 10½" x 6", **$75-125.** Small Dog, 3", **$50-75.**

Poodle, 12½", long and short mohair, jointed, glass eyes, **$100-150.**

Dog, 4", sewn nose and mouth, **$50-75.**

Elephant, 10″ x 13½″, gray felt, red felt saddle, button eyes, tusks, metal wheels, 1885 (M), **$300-400.**

Elephant, 3″ x 5″, gray felt with pins dated 1888, button eyes, rare museum piece, one of a kind (M), **$250-300.**

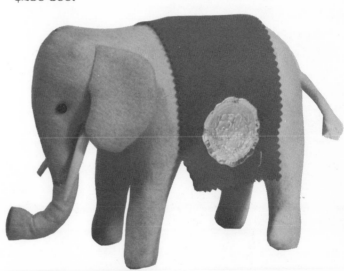

Elephant, 3½″ x 4½″, tan velvet, tusks, 1908 (M), **$100-150.**

Anniversary Elephant, 5″ x 6″, white felt, red saddle, tusks, glass eyes, 1930 (M), **$100-150.**

Elephant, 3″ x 4″, gray velvet, red satin saddle with brass moon on one side and a star on the other, tusks, button eyes (M), 1911, **$150-200.**

Index

About the Authors

Shirley Conway (left) is an antique doll and toy dealer from Huber Heights, Ohio. She first became interested in Steiff toys when she bought a collection and tried to price them. When she discovered that no books had been published on Steiff toys, she decided one was necessary. She now has a shop called Shirley's Carousel. Shirley is a member of the Dayton Doll Study Club of Ohio and United Federation Doll Clubs, Inc.

Jean Wilson (right) is a high school English teacher, antique dealer, and columnist from Piqua, Ohio. She writes a regular column on antiques in the Dayton, Ohio, *Journal Herald* and is a professional writer. Her interest in Steiff toys goes back to the days when she first bought them for her five young sons. Because of her involvement with antiques in general, it was natural that she would collaborate with Shirley on the Steiff book.